L.A. NOIR

**THE CITY
AS CHARACTER**

L.A. NOIR

THE CITY
AS CHARACTER

**ALAIN SILVER &
JAMES URSINI**

**Additional Photography:
ELIZABETH WARD**

SANTA
MONICA
PRESS

To our constant sources of inspiration,
Linda and Dominique.

Published by:
Santa Monica Press LLC
P.O. Box 1076
Santa Monica, CA 90406-1076
1-800-784-9553
www.santamonicapress.com
books@santamonicapress.com

Printed in Canada

Santa Monica Press books are available at special quantity discounts when purchased in bulk by corporations, organizations, or groups. Please call our Special Sales department at 1-800-784-9553.

Library of Congress Cataloging-in-Publication Data

Silver, Alain, 1947-
  L.A. noir : the city as character / by Alain Silver and James Ursini.
     p. cm.
  Filmography: p.
  Includes bibliographical references.
  ISBN 1-59580-006-9
  1. Film noir--United States--History and criticism. 2. Los Angeles (Calif.)--In motion pictures. I. Title: Los Angeles noir. II. Ursini, James. III. Title.
  PN1995.9.F54S57 2005
  791.43'6279494--dc22
                                  2005009681

Cover and interior design by Future Studio

Cover Photograph: Samuel Fuller, facing camera in sunglasses, directs *Crimson Kimono* in Downtown Los Angeles' Little Tokyo.

CONTENTS

Acknowledgments

All the production stills are from the authors' private collection or were provided by David Chierichetti, Samuel Fuller, Walter Hill, Janey Place, and Lee Sanders. They are reproduced courtesy of ABC/Palomar, Columbia, Faces Distributing, MGM, Miramax, Office Kitano, Paramount, RKO, 20th Century-Fox, Tri-Star, United Artists, Universal, and Warner Bros. Individually credited production photographs are by Edward Cronenweth, Elliott Marks, and Darren Michaels. Except as noted in the captions, all the contemporary photographs of Los Angeles are Copyright © 2005 by Alain Silver. A number of photographs were produced in collaboration with Elizabeth Ward, who is the co-creator of *Film Noir: An Encyclopedic Reference to the American Style* and *Raymond Chandler's Los Angeles*. Historical photographs are from the Los Angeles Public Library photo collection. Besides the noir encyclopedia and the Chandler book, our 1999 study of *The Noir Style*, on which we were assisted by Linda Brookover and Robert Porfirio, was extremely influential on the present volume. Lee Sanders helped in researching the locations and Thom Andersen kindly lent us a copy of his documentary feature, *Los Angeles Plays Itself*.

The idea for this book developed over the course of many past projects, not just our jointly written and edited studies of film noir but also in the process of scouting locations for more than a dozen feature films and assorted television series, music videos, and reenactments shot in Los Angeles and its environs over the past 20 years. We are most grateful to all of the co-writers and co-editors of our previous noir books and to the directors, producers, and other filmmakers on the pertinent film and video productions. The experience of making the feature *White Nights* in 2004 at Union Station, around Exposition Park, on Olvera Street, and along Hollywood Boulevard between the Chinese and Pantages theaters provided an operative methodology for the night photography contained herein; in that regard we must acknowledge the work of producer/director of photography Paolo Durazzo.

Some material on *Kiss Me Deadly* is adapted from "KISS ME DEADLY: Evidence of a Style" published in *Film Comment*, Volume 11, number 2 (March–April, 1975) copyright © 1975 by Alain Silver and is reprinted by permission.

Some material on *Gun Crazy* and *Criss Cross* is adapted from "Mad Love" UCLA Film Screening Cooperative Program Notes, May, 1970 copyright © 1970 by Alain Silver and "What is This Thing Called Noir" in *Film Noir Reader*, New York: Limelight Editions, copyright © 1995 by Linda Brookover and Alain Silver and is reprinted by permission.

INTRODUCTION

After the first adaptations of Cain and Chandler, film noir began
to exploit Los Angeles settings in new ways. Geographically,
it shifted increasingly from the Cainian bungalows and suburbs
to the epic dereliction of downtown's Bunker Hill, which
symbolized the rot in the heart of the expanding metropolis . . . . .
Of course, film noir remained an ambiguous aesthetic that
could be manipulated in dramatically different ways.

MIKE DAVIS
City of Quartz

Shooting across the railway viaduct leading into Union Station.

It has been more than a dozen years since Mike Davis described the relationship of film noir and Los Angeles. It's been almost six decades since a couple of French reviewers coined the term to describe the flood of hard-bitten Hollywood productions that were finally allowed to reach Parisian cinemas with the end of World War II. Because those reviewers decided that "black film"—an allusion to a French series featuring translations of novels by Chandler, Cain, and others—was a good epithet, "noir" has become part of the American language. Contemporary writers have used the term to describe dark variants of just about anything from animé to zydeco. In fact, the history of film noir is simple enough. However much aficionados may dicker over specific films, over the consciousness of the filmmakers responsible for the movement, over any particulars, the key films of the classic period are indisputable; they are all any viewer needs to understand what film noir is. While various, oft-cited film and literary movements, from German Expressionist cinema to homegrown detective fiction, may have helped shape the rough beast that is film noir, it slouched toward Los Angeles to be born.

As the city that contains Hollywood, the suburb it annexed in 1910, Los Angeles has a unique position in film history. It is a chameleon metropolis whose features Hollywood filmmakers have attempted to disguise as much as to celebrate. In 1979, the introduction to *Film Noir: An Encyclopedic Reference to the American Style* asserted that the noir cycle was "a self contained reflection of American cultural preoccupations in film form . . . the unique example of a wholly American style." Now, as then, that may seem a hefty claim to make for a group of films that typically focus on characters who are alienated, obsessed, persecuted, and frequently doomed. While the score of books that have examined the noir phenomenon since the *Encyclopedia* may have sustained, challenged, or elaborated on its concepts, from the scope of the classic period to the defining elements of noir, no volume has examined the quintessential dramatic ground of film noir: the city of Los Angeles.

For Raymond Chandler, the preeminent literary chronicler of Los Angeles, who first described its "mean streets" as those down which a man must go, it was a city where one could find both "a special brand of sunshine" and a "wet emptiness," a place that was both "some realtor's dream" and "a mail order city, everything in the catalogue you could get better somewhere else . . . a big hard-boiled city with no more personality than a paper cup." In his penultimate novel *The Long Goodbye* Chandler concluded that Los Angeles was "a city no worse than others, a city rich and vigorous and full of pride, a city lost and beaten and full of emptiness."

Although his work for the studios fattened his wallet many times more rapidly than his books, Chandler's well-documented disdain for Hollywood was rooted in his disapproval of the way its movies homogenized reality, how it removed the hard edge and the stale odor from its subjects. From Chandler's perspective, even the grittiness of the gangster films of the 1930s and the war movies of the next decade was artificial, constructed of stereotypical characters, blank gunshots, and fake blood. Film noir changed all that.

Ironically, despite his script work on *Double Indemnity* (1944) and *The Blue Dahlia* (1946), Chandler never really got it. Film noir took the city he had so vividly described in a score of short stories and novels, took its mean streets, its sunshine, and its wet emptiness, and created a dark and disturbing terrain of apprehension and despair.

"Walking through a city like New York or Los Angeles is like walking through a dream—or a nightmare," writes Nicholas Christopher in *Somewhere in the Night*, and he catalogs elements of that hallucinatory promenade: "Corridors, stairwells, precipitate rooftops, towers, and antennae, streets that can be shadowy or frozen in time or frenetic with flashing steel and chrome, forbidding doorways, gigantic windows that with a subtle change of light can become funhouse mirrors. Not to mention the ever-changing faces and grotesqueries— the city of dreams differs very little from the city of reality." Dream and reality are the touchstones of film noir. Los Angeles is where the filmmakers of the classic period brought these elements together, created the emotional conundrums which the noir protagonist must confront—the land of opportunity and the struggle to get by, the democratic ideal and the political corruption, the American dream and the disaffection of veterans who gave up the best years of their lives.

From its orange groves to its sewers, from Chinatown to the Santa Monica Pier, film noir recruits all that Los Angeles has to offer. Long before television sent images of its

Mike Hammer (Ralph Meeker) pulls his sports car into a Calabasas gas station after picking up the mysterious hitchhiker Christina (Cloris Leachman) in *Kiss Me Deadly*.

city hall, its planetarium, or its oil fields into living rooms around the world, L.A. was the landscape of noir. When wounded insurance agent Walter Neff swerves down Wilshire Boulevard narrowly avoiding a produce truck at the start of *Double Indemnity* or when *The Crimson Kimono* (1959) opens with stripper Sugar Torch being shot down on Main Street, when an aerial shot swoops down onto the parking lot outside a dance club at the beginning of *Criss Cross* (1949), when a wily serial killer fails to escape a dragnet through a maze of storm drains in *He Walked by Night* (1948), as the titles in *Kiss Me Deadly* (1955) scroll past like road signs over a coastal highway, even as the derelict canals and neighborhoods of Venice pass for a seedy border town in *Touch of Evil* (1958), Los Angeles and its environs serve as essential elements in the invocation of the noir mood.

That relationship continues into the 21st century in

neo-noir, the successor genre to the classic period. In his recent feature, *Los Angeles Plays Itself* (2003), documentarian Thom Andersen offers an extended and personal reflection on the complex relationship of Los Angeles and its best known industry, how the city is sometimes background or sometimes character, sometimes masquerading as some other place or sometimes starring as itself. What this book seeks to evoke is the city as a noir character, both in the classic period and the neo-noir genre.

As with all the books we have written or edited on this subject, the text and images of *L.A. Noir* are meant to enhance and never to substitute for the experience of the films themselves. As we suggested in our book on *The Noir Style*, hopefully the words and pictures contained in *L.A. Noir* will lead the reader again or for the first time to watch those movies where the noir ethos and Los Angeles are so intricately entwined.

View of downtown Los Angeles in the 1980s.

This was the final dumping ground.
He thought of Janvier's *Sargasso Sea*.
Just as that imaginary body was a
history of civilization in the form of
a marine junkyard. The studio lot was
one in the form of a dream dump.
A Sargasso of the imagination.

NATHANIEL WEST
The Day of the Locust

HOLLYWOOD:

The Dream Is Born

The dream of "Hollywood" is in many ways just another, slightly more profane version of the American dream, that Puritan ideal of a "city on the hill"—although in this case it is mostly in the flatlands. Hollywood the "idea" was born in 1912 when independent filmmakers like Carl Laemmle, Jesse Lasky, Adolph Zukor, William Fox, Cecil B. DeMille and Thomas Ince decided to escape the legal stranglehold of the Motion Picture Patents Company (Edison, Pathé, Essanay, Méliès, Selig, and Vitagraph). The Patents Company had formed a consortium of the earliest studios in the East and claimed patent ownership on film stock and equipment in an attempt to control production and profits. In response, many filmmakers decided to look as far away as possible for a new more hospitable "back lot." Over the next decade they gradually moved their operations and founded the studios known today as Universal, Paramount, MGM, Fox, and Ince—all originally around the area of today's geographical Hollywood.

With the development of these early studios this once quiet, semi-rural Western town burgeoned into a glamorous metropolis. In less than a decade Hollywood Boulevard, the main street of this new, almost mythical locale, was lined with ornate, exotically named movie palaces like Sid Graumann's Chinese and Egyptian Theaters, plush nightspots like the Montmartre Café and Musso and Frank's, and stylish edifices like the Max Factor Building and the Hollywood Roosevelt Hotel. Over the following decades Hollywood and its many icons, most notably the Hollywood sign, which still looms down from Mt. Lee above it, came to represent to the world the entirety of the American film industry, even after many of the studios had moved to more spacious suburban areas in Culver City and the San Fernando Valley. The word still retained its magic, symbolizing the dream, a dream created by the movies themselves, a dream of glamour, wealth, and fame.

Even as Hollywood the city began to fall on hard times, beginning in the forties and spiraling down from then, it remained a mecca for tourists. Visitors from around the world were undeterred by decaying residential areas, by drug addicts and prostitutes who roamed the star-emblazoned sidewalks of the Walk of Fame, by dream palaces such as the Egyptian or Pantages Theaters closed down or reduced to grind house fare. Still they came, hoping to catch a glimpse of a faded star or match their shoe sizes against those of a dead luminary immortalized in cement in the Chinese Theater's courtyard. The dream was far more resilient and resistant to decay than the actual place.

One of the earliest films to document the decay of the Hollywood dream is *Double Indemnity*, based on the seamy novella by James M. Cain, himself inspired by the real life Snyder-Gray case of 1927 and freely

Neff swerves down Wilshire Boulevard past LaFayette Park at the opening of *Double Indemnity*.

The Spanish colonial Dietrichson house in *Double Indemnity*.

adapted by Billy Wilder and noir novelist Raymond Chandler. From the first night shots of the movie when a wounded Walter Neff (Fred MacMurray) careens through a Hollywood intersection and parks precariously in front of a flat, undistinguished office building on Wilshire Boulevard, the audience knows that they are in an urban landscape far removed from any glamorous vision they might have seen before. As Neff stumbles into his insurance office, past rows and rows of desks where in daytime automaton-like employees sit filing insurance claims and who are now but a ghostly presence, he clutches his wound as he tells the viewer his lurid story.

Neff's narrative is one of greed, sex, and murder—key elements in any tale of corruption. The story within the story begins with a more familiar image of Hollywood for thirties and early-forties audiences—a spacious house set in Los Feliz, once a high class residential neighborhood full of hillside homes of movie celebrities (although the actual house is in the Hollywood Hills). The California sun is shining, and Neff pulls up in front of "one of those California Spanish houses everyone was nuts about 10 or 15 years ago." Inside the house "sunshine coming in through the Venetian blinds showed up the dust in the air." Outside, as he drives away, Neff notices the "smell of honeysuckle all along that street. How could I have known that murder can sometimes smell like honeysuckle?"

This house and its surroundings are the core metaphor of the film. To Neff it contains all the possibilities of the American dream: wealth, love, and beating the system. When a blonde-haired Phyllis Dietrichson (Barbara Stanwyck) first appears on the second floor landing, wrapped in only a towel, Neff is awestruck. When she comes down later to indulge in a bit of classic double entendre, Neff cannot keep his eyes off her dangling foot and its "honey of an anklet," symbolizing not only her sexual power over him but also the wealth for which he so yearns. When, in a second visit, she subtly proposes a get-rich scheme in which they can collect on a double indemnity policy on her older, oppressive husband, Neff is caught in the web of this classic noir spider woman.

But Neff is no mindless dupe. He has his own reasons for his self-confessed crime. As he says to the viewer a little later on, "You're like the guy behind the roulette wheel, watching the customers to make sure they don't crook the house. And then one night, you get to thinking how you could crook the house yourself." He wants the American dream at any cost, even if he has to become a killer. Phyllis represents excitement and opportunity to him. She is sexual, she is romantic in her own perverse way (after all in the final scene she is unable to shoot him a second time even though she is "rotten to the heart"), and she likes the luxuries of life, something Neff has had to do without.

Neff's apartment, where a key love scene is

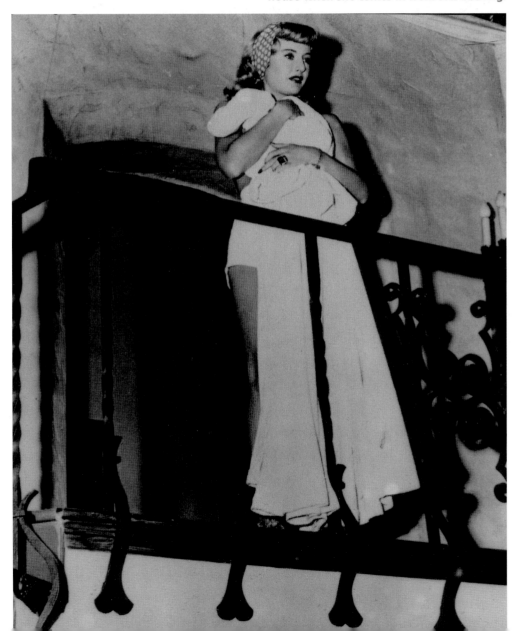

Phyllis Dietrichson (Barbara Stanwyck) first meets Walter Neff in her Spanish colonial house when she comes in from sun bathing.

Phyllis Dietrichson (Barbara Stanwyck) and her husband (Tom Powers) meet with insurance agent Walter Neff (Fred MacMurray) in the living room of their Spanish colonial house.

played out, was modeled by director Billy Wilder after a small, dingy apartment he rented at the Chateau Marmont on Sunset Boulevard when he first arrived in Los Angeles from Germany in the thirties. It stands in stark contrast to the Dietrichson mansion, with its whitewashed Spanish colonial exterior, its expansive, well-lit rooms, and sweeping staircase. Neff's apartment is cramped, shadowy, and spare, much like its bitter, world-weary tenant who seems to have no life outside of his job as an insurance salesman. While his easy, bantering style serves him well in that job, Neff has little enthusiasm for his product or ambitions for advancement. His only friend is his boss Barton Keyes (Edward G. Robinson), for whom he has a deep level of respect but whom he ultimately deceives and betrays for Phyllis and the money.

Once Neff meets Phyllis, they become co-dependents in love and murder, or in Keyes' analogy riders on "a trolley car, and one can't get off without the other. They have to go on riding to the end of the line. And the last stop is the cemetery." For a while at least, before the plan falls apart, Neff feels alive, filled with desire for Phyllis as well as for "crooking the house" and becoming financially independent. Even the furtive meetings between Neff and Phyllis carry an inherent thrill.

When the couple meets in the aisles of Jerry's Market (once located on Vermont Avenue near Franklin Avenue), they are circumspect and cautious,

Phyllis Dietrichson (Barbara Stanwyck) and her husband (Tom Powers) in the foyer after their meeting with insurance agent Walter Neff (Fred MacMurray).

Chateau Marmont Hotel on Sunset Boulevard, Billy Wilder's old room was used as a model for Neff's apartment in *Double Indemnity*.

Phyllis Dietrichson (Barbara Stanwyck) hides behind the door of the apartment of Walter Neff (Fred MacMurray).

**Barton Keyes (Edward G. Robinson, right)
almost catches Phyllis Dietrichson (Barbara
Stanwyck) when he visits Neff's apartment.**

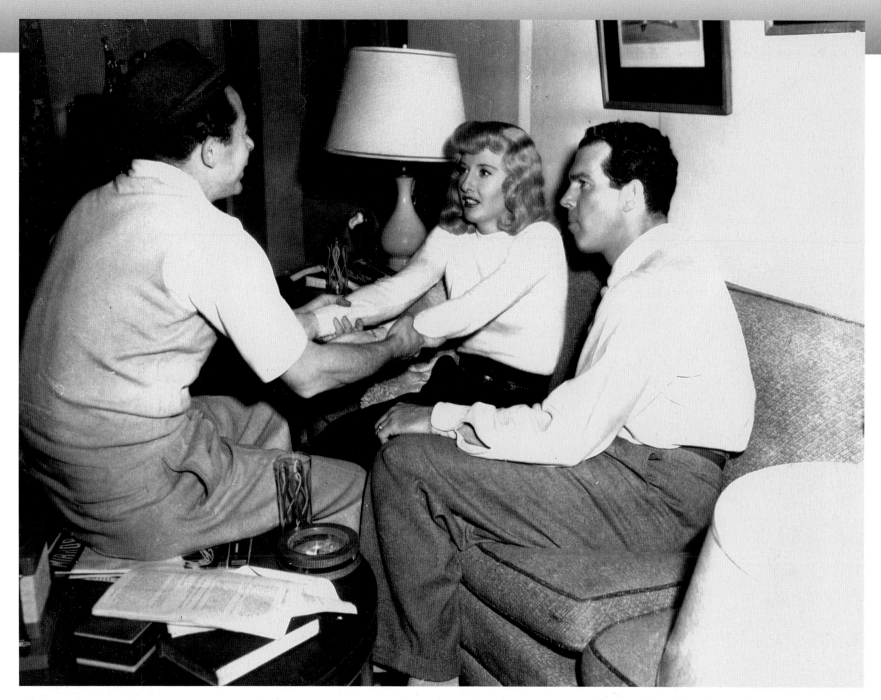

Billy Wilder directs Barbara Stanwyck and Fred MacMurray in the apartment set.

but sexually charged as they are unable even to touch, staring forlornly above the rows of canned and processed foods. When Phyllis visits Neff in his apartment, even though they agreed not to for the duration of the investigation, they embrace even more passionately knowing that they could be under surveillance. And in fact, in the next scene the obsessive Keyes does appear at Neff's door, as Phyllis hides behind it, like teenagers caught in a sexual tryst by their parents. But even as he verifies that everything has gone according to plan, Neff feels the fateful and deadly pull of the force that brings down so many characters in the noir underworld and "suddenly it came over me that everything would go wrong. It sounds crazy, Keyes, but it's true: I couldn't hear my own footsteps. It was the walk of a dead man."

Billy Wilder directs Barbara Stanwyck and Fred MacMurray in Jerry's Market while police officers guard the food, an extremely valuable commodity during World War II rationing, used as set dressing.

After the murder, Phyllis Dietrichson (Barbara Stanwyck) meets Walter Neff (Fred MacMurray) at Jerry's Market.

Pitfall (1948), directed by Andre de Toth, is an even more caustic examination of the American dream than *Double Indemnity,* chiefly because its subject is the post-war nuclear family. The middle-class residential nuclear family of mother, father and 2.4 children is a creation of the post-war corporate world in partnership with the government. This is particularly true of Los Angeles, which was home to the largest industry in the country during World War II, military product development, and almost half of the American aircraft factories such as Douglas Aircraft in Santa Monica. When the war ended so did the desperate need for military products. In response, what Eisenhower would dub the military-industrial complex engineered tax breaks and housing subsidies to create the ideal consuming unit: the residential nuclear family with a working father, purchasing mother, and dependent children, a unit which would buy the new consumer goods the war industries would retool to produce en masse: cars, household appliances, and houses themselves. In Los Angeles, new suburbs were born, including the San Fernando and San Gabriel valleys and the South Bay-Long Beach area.

Pitfall's nuclear family lives in one of the older middle-class areas of Los Angeles: the Hollywood Hills. The film opens with husband, wife, and child at the breakfast table arguing playfully over the minutiae of everyday life, a scene which was repeated endlessly in the fifties on television sitcoms like *Leave It to Beaver* and *Father Knows Best.* But the tone here is different, mainly because of the husband and father, John Forbes (Dick Powell). He is bitter and dissatisfied, a quality entirely absent in the sitcoms, which were designed to promote the ideal suburban nuclear family. He talks about being in a "rut," about going to the same job every day, coming home at the exact same time. He even admonishes his son, "Until my rich uncle dies, quit growing." Although the wife, Sue (Jane Wyatt, who would later portray, ironically, or perhaps not so ironically, the wife and mother in the sitcom *Father Knows Best*) good-naturedly jokes about his unrest and irritability, it is a harbinger of things to come.

Forbes expresses the same sense of futility to his boss at his insurance company, also in Hollywood. He has become a company man, "a little man with a briefcase," as the femme fatale of the piece, Mona Stevens (Lizabeth Scott), will later remark. When working he rarely makes eye contact, focusing entirely on the papers in his ubiquitous briefcase. When he goes to investigate an insurance case involving Mona, it is one of the first things she mocks him about. It is precisely because she reinforces his own sense of who he has become that he is attracted to her.

Forbes ends up accompanying Mona out to Santa Monica Pier to take a ride in a motorboat, which her boyfriend Bill Smiley (Byron Barr) has purchased with purloined money and which Forbes' company may

Sue Forbes (Jane Wyatt) and son Tommy (Jimmy Hunt) comfort
John Forbes (Dick Powell) in their Hollywood Hills home.

soon be trying to repossess. Already entranced by her intelligence and perceptiveness, Forbes is caught up in her sense of excitement, externalized by the abandon with which she drives the boat.

Mona is no standard femme fatale. In fact she is something of an anti-femme fatale. Rather than exhibiting a sense of self-possession and power, when faced with the loss of her boat, she is forlorn and resigned. She is a classic female victim, attracted to men who will hurt her, not just the convicted and imprisoned Smiley but to Forbes as well. She never

questions him concerning his personal life before they have a one-night stand. Even her body language radiates "victim." Her head is often down, her eyes downcast, her posture bent, even when she models dresses at the May Company, which at that time was a department store for the upper middle class much like the more celebrated Bullocks, a bit farther east. Ironically, Mona works in a place wearing dresses and surrounded by other goods which she cannot afford. Although she tries to maintain her "runway" image off the job she lacks the confidence to pull it off. The irony of her status is compounded when Mac (played as always with great subtlety by Raymond Burr), the private investigator whom Forbes hired and who is stalking her, comes into the store to harass her.

The filmmakers make it clear that their emotional sympathy is with Mona. While a chastened Forbes runs back to the safety of his middle-class home after his brief interlude with her, Mona is left to face a stalker and a jealous boyfriend, who is about to be released from jail. Whatever sympathies the audience might have had for Forbes at the beginning (despite his "walk on the wild side,") slowly dissolve as he continues to deceive his wife about the affair. He is beaten up by his own employee, the defiant and jealous Mac, and his

Former department store, the May Company, on Wilshire Boulevard at Fairfax Avenue (now part of the Los Angeles County Museum of Art) where Mona works as a model in *Pitfall*.

cowardice eventually leads to the death of two men: Smiley is mistaken for a prowler and shot by Forbes and, convinced that he now has the power to coerce her, Mac is shot by Mona as he attempts to abduct her. When Forbes faces questioning by the police at the Hall of Justice downtown with that imposing symbol of authority of so many noirs, the City Hall, looming in the background, they express their disgust with Forbes, telling him in no uncertain terms that he should be the one locked up, not Mona. A chastened Forbes returns to his now-dysfunctional family with an uncertain future. Within its very limited budget and running time, *Pitfall* exposes—as only a noir film can—the soft center of the American social ideal.

Sunset Boulevard (1950) is in many ways a companion piece to *Double Indemnity*. Its subject, too, is the American dream; but rather than just being set in Hollywood, it is about Hollywood as an idea and a place. The film opens on the central symbol of the film: silent film star Norma Desmond's (Gloria Swanson) "great big house" on Sunset Boulevard (although the actual house belonged to the wife of oil magnate J. Paul Getty and was on Wilshire Boulevard near Irving). It is a classic movie mansion, as presented by director Billy Wilder and cinematographer John F. Seitz. Seitz also shot *Double Indemnity* and was known for his development of the "chiaroscuro" style of shooting beginning in the twenties when he worked with visionary director Rex Ingram. This shadowy style, a lynchpin of film

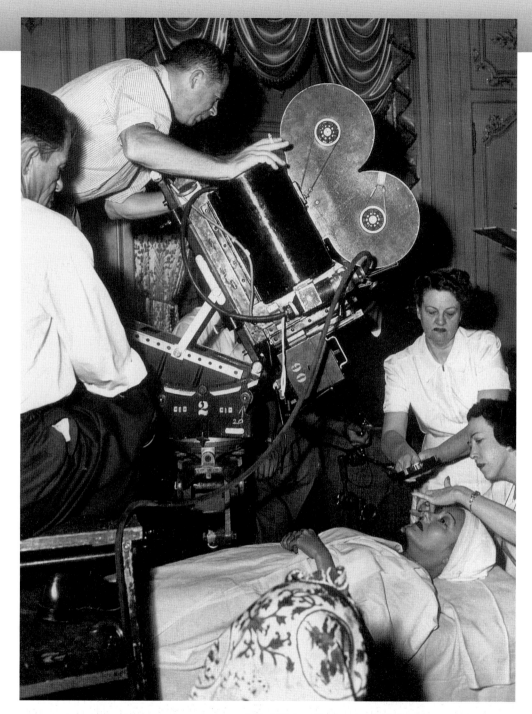

Billy Wilder directs the facial at Norma Desmond's (Gloria Swanson) Sunset Boulevard mansion.

noir, is used to great effect in all of Seitz's work at Paramount for Wilder and other directors.

Most of the scenes at the mansion are at night, with extensive use of dark and light patterns, as is appropriate for this almost Gothic abode in the tradition of Emily Brontë's *Wuthering Heights* and her sister Charlotte's *Jane Eyre*. It is here that Norma Desmond hides from the world, living among the cluttered memories of the past. She has a pool, clubhouse, and many other amenities, all now unused as she spends almost all of her time watching silent movies of herself. Actors "didn't need dialogue. We had faces then," is Norma's celebrated pronouncement about the state of movies in 1950. She also works sporadically on a rambling, incoherent comeback script called *Salome*. Her only companions are her monkey, which she eventually buries in the backyard, and her servant/ex-husband/ex-director (Erich von Stroheim), whose job it is to cater to her every whim and keep up the illusion that the world still remembers her by forging fan letters. One of the subtle ironies is that, while never married to Swanson, Stroheim was fired as director of *Queen Kelly* by its producer, Swanson's paramour Joe Kennedy. Wilder used clips of this picture in Desmond's home theater.

Into this movie museum stumbles the cynical, broke Hollywood writer of a new generation, uninter-

Norma Desmond (Gloria Swanson) visits Cecil B. DeMille on a soundstage at Paramount studios.

ested in cinema history, but always looking for an angle by which he can turn a few dollars. The audience first sees Joe Gillis (William Holden) dead, floating in a pool, as he begins to narrate his story from his watery grave. Allowing a dead character to narrate was certainly a controversial narrative format when Wilder first proposed it to Paramount, but since first-person narration had become a staple of film noir and *Double Indemnity* had been extremely successful in that mode, they readily agreed.

Central to any understanding of the character of Gillis is the apartment he lives in before Norma: the Alto Nido Apartments at the top of Ivar Avenue in Hollywood. By this time, Hollywood itself was already on the edge of a slippery slope. Once well-kept apartment buildings like the Alto Nido (literally a "high nest") were becoming low-rent, semi-transient abodes. In this spare, cramped space Gillis tries to hide from his creditors while he pounds out a new script, hoping the studio will pay him enough to dig himself out of debt. Soon, however, he finds himself pursued by repo men. When they chase him and his car blows a tire, he manages to slip unseen into Norma's driveway.

The sexual/financial relationship that develops between the aging star and the young writer epitomizes the conflicting viewpoints of old Hollywood and new Hollywood. Joe becomes not only her lover but her collaborator as well. He works on her unwieldy script rather reluctantly and only because

The apartments above Franklin Avenue where Joe Gillis lives in *Sunset Boulevard*.

Joe Gillis (William Holden) rewrites Norma Desmond's (Gloria Swanson) script in a garage room at her Sunset Boulevard mansion.

Joe Gillis
(William Holden)
with Norma
Desmond (Gloria
Swanson) at her
exclusive New
Year's party.

she is supporting him and promises that her old direc- tor Cecil B. DeMille (who portrays himself and really was one of Swanson's directors in the twenties) will produce it. At this point, as he spends more time with her, Gillis is caught up in her illusions. Only when he escapes her emotional entrapment—exemplified by the scenes on the couch where she imprisons him physically with her body—to attend a party of his young movie-business friends does Joe feel embar- rassed over being a gigolo.

Billy Wilder directs the final "press conference" scene at Norma Desmond's Sunset Boulevard mansion.

These awkward encounters happen first at Schwab's Drugstore (the famed Hollywood hangout on Sunset Boulevard near Crescent Heights Boulevard, no longer there) and again on the Paramount lot. There he meets the idealistic Betty Schaefer (Nancy Olson), a secretary and would-be writer who wants to develop a story that Joe has pitched to her boss as a quality script. Convinced that he should give it a shot, Joe sneaks out to work with her and falls in love with his new collaborator.

Joe Gillis (William Holden) discusses script ideas with Betty Schaefer (Nancy Olson) outside of the writer's building on the Paramount lot.

The climax of the movie is bifocal. When Norma drives onto the Paramount lot to see DeMille—not realizing that an assistant had called about renting her car—she must confront the new world of Hollywood and cannot escape the realization that this is not her

The Bronson drive-in gate at Paramount studios in the 1980s.

Max von Mayerling (Erich von Stroheim) directs a crazed Norma Desmond (Gloria Swanson) at her Mansion press conference after Gillis' murder.

universe anymore. When she finds out that Joe has been emotionally unfaithful with Betty, Norma's carefully constructed world begins to collapse. No longer isolated within her Gothic mansion, Norma loses her mind and shoots Joe. As the audience watches Joe's body being unceremoniously fished out of the pool, Norma waits in her world of illusion. She gets her legendary "close-up" as she descends the sweeping staircase of her mansion in the final scene. The cameras are not those of DeMille's crew but a score of newsreel cameramen recording her descent into complete madness.

Leigh Brackett, who also collaborated on the screenplay for Chandler's *The Big Sleep* in 1946, wrote Robert Altman's adaptation of Raymond Chandler's *The Long Goodbye* (1973, further discussed in the next chapter). Unlike *The Big Sleep* and *Murder, My Sweet* (1944), which were shot almost entirely on studio sets, Altman used actual locations to capture a sense of Los Angeles and the point of view of one of its most celebrated chroniclers, Raymond Chandler. Chandler understood Los Angeles as only an immigrant could. Like Billy Wilder, who introduced him to screenwriting on *Double Indemnity,* Chandler had a conflicted relationship with Hollywood. Not having been raised in the glamour and glitz of the city, Chandler's depiction of its dark side ultimately became outright hatred for

The Long Goodbye: Gangster Marty Augustine (Mark Rydell) confronts Philip Marlowe (Elliott Gould) outside his apartment on High Tower Drive in Hollywood.

the movies and the business of making them. In this updated version of the 1953 novel, Marlowe (Elliott Gould) buys cat food at an all-night market in the flat-lands and lives in an Italianate apartment complex near the Hollywood Bowl—the High Tower Apartments off Highland Avenue. It is a classic Hollywood building, eclectic and unabashed in its display of multiple architectural styles. Its inhabitants, however, with the exception of Marlowe, are strictly post-sixties Hollywood; the neighbors are beautiful young women who seem most concerned with yoga, meditation, and improving their tanned and toned California bodies. They liltingly greet Marlowe, like a

All-night market on Fountain Avenue where Marlowe buys cat food in *The Long Goodbye*.

group of urban sirens, but it is clear he does not understand them.

What Marlowe does understand is the world of murder, corruption, and physical intimidation. He is jailed in the Lincoln Heights facility, a favorite location of Hollywood filmmakers, by cops who think he is withholding information. He is verbally and physically abused by Augustine (Mark Rydell), a mobster looking for a stolen cache of money. He is hit by a car as he pursues a deceptive client down a Hollywood street. Even

Campanile-style elevator of the apartments on High Tower Drive.

though Marlowe sustains heavy damage from all these experiences, he survives, like Chandler's sardonic "knight-errant," to do the right thing.

Impulse (1990, directed by Sondra Locke) opens with one of the most telling images of the decay of Hollywood. It is night. The streets are wet in classic noir style, reflecting the neon signs of the cheap motels that line Sunset Boulevard and Las Palmas Avenue. Most of them cater to hookers and drug addicts. On the deserted street the viewer sees the lone figure of a prostitute. She is dressed in a skin tight, faux animal skin mini dress, stiletto heels, and an obvious wig. She is approached by a "john" who wants a "date." She agrees to the transaction and leads him to a motel. Once they are near the room, the john begins to rough her up as part of the sex play. But before he can gratify his sadistic desires, the vice squad breaks in and arrests him. This opening sequence is much grimmer than any vision of Wilder or Chandler. There are no old Hollywood landmarks, no decaying mansions, no smell of honeysuckle. It's all drug dealing, violence, and sex for sale.

Within a few minutes it is revealed that the prostitute is actually undercover vice cop Lottie Mason (Theresa Russell), whose job is to seduce men and then call in reinforcements after they commit a bookable offense. Lottie is a typical neo-noir protagonist: broke, desperate, and bitter about her work in the urban jungle of Hollywood. She is also an *atypical* noir figure;

Location from *Impulse* at Sunset Boulevard as it appears today.

Undercover policewoman Lottie Mason (Theresa Russell) walks down Sunset Boulevard at Las Palmas Avenue.

she is a female protagonist, not an antagonistic femme fatale like Phyllis Dietrichson or Anna in *Criss Cross*. Like the secretary-turned-detective Carol "Kansas" Richman (Ella Raines) in *Phantom Lady* (1944), Lottie begins as an idealist. Although she never becomes a Marlowe or Sam Spade in vinyl and heels, she holds her own in the male-dominated police force of the eighties, an empowered woman warrior liberated by the feminist movement of the decade before, even as she masquerades in an underworld where women are pure sex objects.

But with all her snappy repartee, despite her deftness with her oversized gun and muscle car (both phallic symbols that she co-opts from the male world), she is still a victim. She plays a prostitute who caters to men and is so convincing at it that she begins to identify with the role. At one point she agrees, for a large sum of money, to go to a drug dealer's modern mansion off Sunset Boulevard. Here, in the hills above the urban sprawl, she can live a fantasy for a few moments.

Even when isolated physically from the jungle below, Lottie still personifies noir's class-conscious view of the universe. She tells her psychiatrist, who has been assigned by Internal Affairs to measure her emotional stability, that she likes the power she has over men when she plays a hooker. Ultimately, however, it is the men who have the power, the money, and the influence. In these transitory phantom relation-

ships, she learns over and over again that the underlying dynamic is one of violence and exploitation. She is even a victim at work, sexually harassed by a lecherous fellow cop, Morgan (George Dzundza), whom she refuses to report out of a sense of futility. She uses the Laurelwood, her secluded apartment on the edge of Hollywood near Studio City, as a refuge from the world. Even there she is pursed by demons that contribute to her victimization—failed relationships, bill collectors, and eventually her nemesis Morgan, who invades her sanctuary.

What makes this film powerful is that it offers no pat answers for Lottie. She forms an on-and-off relationship with a more sensitive male in the person of Stan (Jeff Fahey), a lawyer working for the district attorney. But she cannot trust any man: Stan gets drunk and beats her for hiding information from him. In the final scene of the movie, set at Los Angeles International Airport, she reconciles with Stan after returning the money stolen from the drug dealer. This is anything but a happy ending in the traditional, Hollywood manner. She is still trapped in Los Angeles, without the money she took to escape the city, and still haunted by her sense of alienation and futility.

In the manner of Robert Towne's scripts to *Chinatown* (1974) and its sequel *The Two Jakes* (1990), *L.A. Confidential* (1997), based on a novel by James Ellroy and scripted by Brian Helgeland and Curtis Hanson, uses certain events inspired by fact as a narrative core. Also a period film, *L.A. Confidential* is set in 1953, the heart of the classic period of film noir, the year of release for *The Big Heat* and *Vicki*. The ambitious, self-righteous, and obsessed cops of *L.A. Confidential* recall the fictional detectives portrayed by Glenn Ford and Richard Boone in the aforemen-

tioned movies. Despite director Curtis Hanson's assertion that he did not want the picture to be an "homage to a style from the past or neo-noir," *L.A. Confidential* is full of many overt references to the noir style and the noir era. Lynn Bracken (Kim Basinger), the femme fatale of the piece, is part of a stable of high-class hook-

Restaurant adjacent to Warner Hollywood studios, formerly Samuel Goldwyn, featured in *L.A. Confidential*.

**Lynn Bracken (Kim Basinger) entertains L.A.P.D.
Detective Bud White (Russell Crowe) . . . or vice-versa.**

Bar just east of Hollywood and Vine, adjacent to the Pantages theater (and just south of the Capitol Records Building), featured in *L.A. Confidential*.

Crossroads of the World, where the office of Sid Hudgens (Danny DeVito) is located in *L.A. Confidential*.

ers who resemble the glamorous actresses of the era. In one scene, she entertains a local councilman by projecting a 16mm print of *This Gun for Hire,* which stars her look-alike, Veronica Lake. When not serving as tipster for a scandal mag, narcotics detective Jack Vincennes (Kevin Spacey) is technical advisor for a fictional TV series modeled on *Dragnet.*

In this context of self-conscious allusions, director Hanson found locations that reflect both the real city and the fictionalized city of the period. Ironically, one of the most striking sequences in terms of topography—Vincennes' arrest of a young actor just down the street from where searchlights accompany a

movie premiere at the "El Cortez" theater on Hollywood Boulevard—features a location that does not exist. An equally ironic and throwaway moment with Vincennes comes later as he exits the Frolic Room on Hollywood Boulevard and the marquee on the Pantages Theater behind him is for *The Bad and the Beautiful,* Vincente Minnelli's MGM melodrama about filmmakers.

Throughout the narrative, Hanson alternates location types, switching between the monumental and everyday. The steps of City Hall and the neo-Baroque fixtures of the Pacific Electric Building, out of which tough cop Bud White (Russell Crowe) dangles a recalcitrant district attorney, contrast vividly with the run-down clapboard of the derelict craftsmen houses of Echo Park and South Central. The power brokers live in the upscale homes, such as Richard Neutra's Lovell House, and exploit women such as Lynn, who live in modest but well-kept Spanish moderns in the Larchmont district. Characters die at the Hollywood Center Motel on Sunset Boulevard, a few steps from the one frequented by vice cop Lottie Mason in *Impulse*, or at the Night Owl Coffee Shop on 6th, just two blocks from Downtown's skid row and a stone's throw from where Sugar Torch is gunned down in *Crimson Kimono*. The office of Sid Hudgens is in Crossroads of the World, a

The Hollywood Athletic Club on Sunset Boulevard, where Hammer finds the "great whatsit" in a locker in *Kiss Me Deadly*.

streamline moderne "mini-mall" from 1937 that features a central building shaped like a ship with a spinning globe atop a spire. A block east along Sunset is the Hollywood Athletic Club, where Mike Hammer in *Kiss Me Deadly* finds the hot box known as the "great whatsit" in a locker (more on this picture in Chapters Two and Three).

Mulholland Drive (2001) is present-day Hollywood in the final stages of decay. It is the most caustic attack on the ethos of Hollywood since Nathaniel West's tormented narrative in *The Day of the Locust* in 1939. As in West's novel, director David Lynch turns Hollywood into a surreal nightmare of greed, lust, betrayal, jealousy, and hypocrisy. It is the story of struggling actress Diane Selwyn (Naomi Watts) who, like the protagonists in Lynch's other noir-influenced stories *Blue Velvet* and *Lost Highway*, leads a schizophrenic life, half-real, half-dream. In the early part of the movie the audience sees Diane (in her dream form, "Betty") arriving at LAX from the "heartland." She is full of middle-American aspirations and naiveté. Diane/Betty is accompanied by a pair of elderly, seemingly benign residents of Los Angeles who are returning home. They welcome her to their city effusively, almost excessively. It is significant that these two surrogate grandparents become the demons who drive her to suicide in the final scenes. Like the icons of Hollywood which Lynch incorporates into the story—the Hollywood sign; Mulholland Drive; Sunset

The "Snow White" Apartments in Los Feliz, home to Diane Selwyn in Mulholland Drive.

Boulevard; the fantasy cottages in Los Feliz, which were part of the original Disney Studios and which stand in for Diane's apartment complex in West Hollywood; the Paramount Gate; the aerial vistas of downtown Hollywood; the classic diners (although Winkie's on Sunset in the movie is actually Caesar's in Gardena)—these pseudo-grandparents symbolize the schizophrenic and hypocritical entity which is "tinsel town."

As "Betty," Diana finds herself involved with a classic femme fatale—Rita (Laura Herring), who has been in an accident off Mulholland Drive above Sunset Boulevard and wandered in a daze into the Spanish courtyard apartment of Betty's aunt. Rita is the reincarnation of Rita Hayworth in *Gilda*, whom she sees on a poster before assuming the name. Her sultry looks and voluptuous figure are irresistible to the innocent Betty, and they become lovers. In the dream form of this relationship the love is as tender as any forties fiction. Betty takes the lead as she assists the amnesiac Rita in her search for her true identity, echoing another common theme in classic noir.

But when the film relocates from the dream to Diane's "real" life in the last part of the movie, the audience realizes that Rita, whose "real" name is Camilla, is the dominant one. She taunts her ex-lover

Rita/Camilla (Laura Harring, left) meets Betty/Diane
(Naomi Watts) at "Winkie's" on Sunset Boulevard
(shot at Caesar's in the South Bay).

Diane with her new fiancé, the director Adam Kesher (Justin Theroux), as well as other female lovers. The dream world Diane creates is as comforting as a Nancy Drew mystery as the two girls go hunting for the key, literally and figuratively in this case, to the crime and, in the process, become fast friends. In Lynch's dark vision, Camilla betrays Diane at a party in the director's house off Mulholland Drive, a party where all the persons who Diane has incorporated into her dream world are revealed to the audience, in a pointedly noir spin on Hollywood's supreme example of dream-making, *The Wizard of Oz*.

Caesar's Restaurant, which acts as Winkie's in *Mulholland Drive*.

There is also a connecting parallel plot in Mulholland Drive that revolves around the director. In this context, Lynch has free reign to paint the movie industry with black humor and surrealist touches. It is a business run by sociopathic mafiosi. Dwarves in isolated chambers control production companies such as Ryan Entertainment (which is housed downtown in the ornate Banks Huntley Building). Mysterious movie cowboys can compel a director to meet in Beachwood Canyon above Franklin Avenue and do their bidding. It is an industry that has very little to do with art. And even would-be artists, like the director, are cowardly

Hollywood and downtown in the distance seen from above the Cahuenga Pass.

poseurs with trendy thick-rimmed glasses who carry golf clubs to meetings.

Diane creates her own little movie in her head, not much worse or much better than the average Hollywood fare, filled with suspense, beautiful mysterious women, and unexplained plot points. When, Alice-like, the insertion of an enigmatic blue key drives her back into reality, she is destroyed by the faithlessness and mockery of her colleagues. The party at the director's hillside estate is the moment that breaks her spirit totally.

There, after witnessing Camilla flirting with her multiple lovers, she breaks down like the performer she and Rita visited in her dream, shot at the Tower Theater downtown, who sings plaintively in Spanish the Roy Orbison hit "Crying." The evercreative Diane then concocts another bit of drama by hiring a hit man to eliminate Camilla, but it's too late. The loss and guilt lead to figurative self-immolation and the inevitable headlines which proclaim a "true" Hollywood story: "Starlet found dead in quaint historical Hollywood apartment." Lynch returns to the opening image of the movie—the decaying body of a woman—and adds a layer of irony by superimposing overlit shots of Betty and Rita, happy and laughing, their shadows thrown on a noir screen by a city that destroys its dreamers.

Site of the fictional "Club Silencio" in *Mulholland Drive*.

2

On thinking about Hell, I gather
My brother Shelley found it was a place
Much like the city of London. I
Who live in Los Angeles and not in London
Find, on thinking about Hell, that it must be
Still more like Los Angeles.

BERTOLT BRECHT

THE WESTSIDE AND THE COAST:

Where the Dream Runs Out of Steam

. . . if the darkness and corruption leave
A vestige of the thoughts that once I had.

CHRISTINA ROSSETTI, "Remember"
quoted in *Kiss Me Deadly*

Director Edward Dmytryk outside Schwab's on Sunset Boulevard in the 1940s.

Film noir has always been about class struggle, which is small wonder considering the political leanings of so many of the participants in the cycle. Edward Dmytryk (*Murder, My Sweet; Cornered*), Elia Kazan (*Boomerang, Panic in the Streets*), Albert Maltz (*This Gun for Hire, The Naked City*), Daniel Mainwaring (*Out of the Past, The Hitchhiker*), Joseph Losey (*M, The Big Night*), Jules Dassin (*Night and the City, Thieves' Highway*), Dalton Trumbo (*Gun Crazy, The Prowler*), and Abraham Polonsky (*Force of Evil, Body and Soul*) are just a few of the directors and writers who were either blacklisted or gray-listed for periods of their careers during the Eisenhower-McCarthy fifties as discussed in detail in such studies as *The Inquisition in Hollywood.* Consequently, many of noir's creators were involved in progressive movements in the thirties, and with the Second World War and the real threat of fascism, their activism intensified. The horrors of the war further accelerated a sense of urgency in these filmmakers to reveal the corruption and inequities in the capitalist system so that the United States might better fight the creeping evil of fascism. As a result, alongside a deep streak of fatalism that characterizes most of film noir, there also exists this desire to expose social injustice in the hope that it might inspire people to change society.

Los Angeles is visually ideal for externalizing this dichotomous view of the world. It is the "land of sunshine," where the weather is mild year round, one of the reasons filmmakers abandoned cities of the East from New York to Chicago. But underneath that sunshine, writers from Raymond Chandler (*The Big Sleep, Farewell, My Lovely*) and James M. Cain (*Mildred Pierce, Double Indemnity*) to Walter Mosley (*Devil in a Blue Dress, Little Scarlet*) and Joan Didion (*The White Album, Where I Was From*) have discovered the "darkness and corruption" in Los Angeles. And nowhere is this dialectic split more evident than in the geographical division between the Westside and Eastside sections of the city.

The Westside of Los Angeles stretches from the unofficial dividing line between west and east, between rich and poor: Crescent Heights Boulevard. It includes such luxurious communities as Bel-Air, Brentwood, Pacific Palisades; the exclusive incorporated enclave of Beverly Hills; and up the coast highway, Malibu and its private colony stretching to the county line. In these places the elite of the movie industry and of business have made their homes. Beverly Hills was defined when silent film stars Mary Pickford and Douglas Fairbanks built Picfair, their "mansion on the hill." Malibu Colony, the gated and guarded community along the shore, was developed just a few years later when a boat or train was more reliable than the highway for commuting to Hollywood.

As symbols of Hollywood glamour, the Westside is unparalleled. The city of Santa Monica, on which Chandler modeled the corrupt "Bay City," was a beach town where summer cottages provided a weekend escape from the downtown heat. The Santa Monica pier with its amusement park and ballroom, built by developer Charles Looff in 1917, anchored the attractions for resident and tourist alike, an expanse of beach and surf covering that ran south all the way to Palos Verdes. Immediately south is the fantasy community of Venice, the wet dream of Abbot Kinney who was intent on creating a replica of the city's Italian namesake, replete with canals, gondolas, and narrow bridges. Although Kinney's dream fell on hard times in the fifties when the area became a refuge for beats, hippies, and druggies, it has recently undergone a gentrification and now multi-million dollar homes line the refurbished canals.

As the classic period of film noir began, this dreamlike landscape of the Westside, the coast, and the Pacific waters, had become a refuge for the cream of European writers fleeing the anti-Semitic Nazi regime and World War II, including Bertolt Brecht, Aldous Huxley, Thomas Mann, and Christopher Isherwood. Years later in his essay "Hyperion to a Satyr," Huxley vividly described the sunshine/corruption dichotomy when he recalled, "I took a walk with Thomas Mann on a beach some fifteen or twenty miles southwest of Los Angeles. Between the breakers and the highway stretched a broad band of sand, smooth, gently sloping . . . Gone was the congestion of Santa Monica and Venice. Hardly a house was to be seen." What Huxley soon discovered glistening above the pristine sands of what is now Dockweiler Beach— where still hardly a house is to be seen because the postwar tracts were knocked down when LAX expanded—were thousands of condoms spewed out by the Hyperion sewage treatment plant.

Politically, the Westside has also been a major player in the ever-shifting political alignments in Los Angeles, what social historian Mike Davis calls the "power lines." The Westside was built with money from several sources. Real estate speculation began early and boomed in mid-century led by such men as financier Howard Ahmanson, savings and loan magnate Bart Lytton, and, later, developer Eli Broad. The war-bloated aerospace industries followed, centered around Douglas Aircraft, which once occupied all the area around present-day Santa Monica Airport. Lastly, political machines crafted by special interests carved out sections. Before the war, WASPish old money built restricted beach clubs below the Santa Monica palisades. As Mike Davis asserts, in the sixties the more liberal, Westside monied interests, some Christian, some Jewish (Davis' "Jewish" prototype, reformist Republican, savings and loan tycoon Howard Ahmanson Sr. was actually a Methodist) joined with East Los Angeles and South Central Latino and African-American politicos, like future five-term mayor Tom Bradley, and seized control of the city. The corruption of Los Angeles in the thirties bred reformers both liberal and conservative, but Bradley's defeat in 1973 of reactionary mayor Sam Yorty and his avid, largely Republican supporters from the upscale suburbs began a period of real estate development and gentrification that continues as we write. The changes in downtown, Hollywood, and—most dramatically—the Westside are controversial to this day.

Against this backdrop of the Westside and its wealth, noir films from *Mildred Pierce* (1945) to *Touch of Evil* critically examined the concept of "paradise by

the sea" as Abbot Kinney called it. In the opening sequence of *Mildred Pierce*, adapted from the novel by James M. Cain, the title character (played by Joan Crawford, a model of the new professional woman of the forties) finds herself on a pier—partially shot at Santa Monica Pier, partially on a stage set—wrapped in fur and staring out at the dark ocean. She has come there to find some release and redemption and to tell her story of darkness and corruption in the sunny environs of Los Angeles. Her fur represents the class she has worked diligently to become part of, only to find her

Left: The front of the Santa Monica Pier.

Center: Santa Monica Bay from Will Rogers State Beach.

life blighted by murder and betrayal. Although the film itself was shot largely on the studio lot of Warner Brothers, the story sets up the locations of the Westside and its oceanfront as a source of decadence. Monte Beragon (Zachary Scott), the indolent heir and unfaithful husband, has a beach house on the ocean, where he is murdered by Mildred's spoiled daughter Veda (Ann Blyth), who is also having an affair with him.

In Cain's sordid tale of quasi-incest and mother love, Mildred tries to take the blame for the murder, but the real culprit is real estate development.

Mildred's first husband, the weak-willed Bert (Bruce Bennett), fails at his attempts to become a real estate magnate. His deals on the Westside and in Glendale, where he and Mildred live, fail miserably. In the mode of Rosie the Riveter, the new working woman of the Second World War, Mildred takes the reins and claws her way into the restaurant business using Monte's inherited wealth as a platform. But this enterprise also goes broke, as Monte continues to live high while Mildred tries to hold her chain of restaurants together.

Significantly, the murder of Monte by Velda is

The entrance arch to the Santa Monica Pier at dusk in the 1980s. Even the Westside is not exempt from decay as evidenced by the malfunctioning neon letters.

Mildred Pierce (Joan Crawford) is questioned by a police officer on the Santa Monica Pier.

played out in his beach house, the supposed scene of their trysts, with its moderne style. Like the Malibu beach house in Robert Aldrich's adaptation *Kiss Me Deadly*, Huxley's serene space "between the breakers and the highway" becomes a noir location. Seen at night with chiaroscuro shadows typical of noir style, the "smooth, gently sloping" beach cannot restrain the decay below the surface from emerging. Rich or poor, malignant or merely misguided, none can escape the pull of the noir undertide by the L.A. seashore, where the dream finally runs out of room.

Gun Crazy (1950) is shot almost entirely in Los Angeles County, even though a number of the locations stand in for other cities. For instance, the celebrated one-take Hampton bank robbery shot from the back seat of a Cadillac was staged in Montrose, a suburb of Los Angeles. The robbery of the meatpacking factory purportedly in New Mexico was actually set at the now-defunct Armour facility in the South Bay. *Gun Crazy* is the supreme example of what director Luis Buñuel and the surrealists called *amour fou,* "mad love," which critic Raymond Durgnat described in his book on Buñuel as "the love which, acting out rather than smoothing over all its torments and ambivalences, defying all the distractions and obstacles posed by the world, casts aside all scruples, all calculations and all egoistic restraint."

Male protagonist, Bart Tare (John Dall), spots Annie Laurie Starr (Peggy Cummins) in a sideshow attraction where she demonstrates her adept gunplay, and is immediately hooked. An erotic, explosive, and powerful woman who shares his gun-craziness is something this conflicted young man has never seen. The first shot of Annie Laurie Starr is from a low angle as she strides into the frame firing two pistols above her head. Bart's love/hate relationship with guns quickly

Bart Tare (John Dahl) and Annie Laurie Starr (Peggy Cummins) after a robbery.

transfers to Laurie. Bart gets a job with the carnival, and from then on, Laurie wears her beret at an angle, her sweaters tight, and her lipstick thick. When a jealous sideshow manager fires them both, Laurie convinces Bart that there is more money to be had by staging shooting exhibitions in banks rather than tents. Their short-lived crime spree/love affair takes them across the West where every robbery gives Laurie such an adrenalin rush that the afterglow is unmistakably sexual. Annie plays the more traditional aggressive male role, always pushing Bart to further heights sexually and criminally, while Bart takes a submissive position, trying to restrain and reason with the stubborn Annie.

As they race off from the Hampton bank, Laurie looks back, her hands around Bart's neck as if to embrace him. In that sustained, breathless glance backwards toward the camera, the sexual thrill is more important than the money. By today's standards, mere innuendo of sexual gratification from a criminal act is rather tame. Director Joe Lewis' staging of this scene in *Gun Crazy*, the tightly controlled perspective from the back of the car and the entire sequence shot without a cut, creates a tension for the viewer that is entirely analogous to the couple's. The release of the tension is keyed to Laurie's expression. What is building, to use more contemporary terminology, is an addiction. Laurie's addiction to violence, initially motivated by the desire for "money and all the things it will buy," is now an irresistible urge. In feeding her habit, Bart is a typical codependent. In another classic scene, Bart and Annie decide to break up in order to avoid the police. They start to speed off in separate cars, but suddenly both cars turn back as if magnetically drawn and the two lovers reunite, unable to separate even for a short period of time because as Bart somewhat ruefully observes, "We go together. I don't know how. Maybe like guns and ammunition go together."

The lovers' relationship is not entirely violent and sexual. There is a romantic, idyllic sequence in which the dangerous duo takes a hiatus from crime and decides to act like a "normal couple." The scene is Santa Monica in a low-rent hotel that features a view of the pier in the background in a process shot. They spend this time visiting the arcade on the pier—used many times in later noir films from *Quicksand* and *Dark Corner* (where it masquerades as an East Coast amusement park) to *Farewell, My Lovely* and *They Shoot Horses, Don't They?* They dance in the famous La Monica Ballroom and walk along the railing by the ocean. It is as if the couple is trying to imitate the actions of normal lovers in this resort setting where thousands come each year to find romance and escape. They seem almost desperate to become like the lovers who surround them in the ballroom; but neither is made for that life. Drawn to danger and excitement, as explosive as guns and bullets, they are trapped in the transgressive cycle of *amour fou.*

Quicksand (1950), starring Mickey Rooney as Dan Brady, presents a side of Santa Monica and the Westside rarely seen on the screen. Rather than centering on the communities of the rich and famous, this film gives the viewer a peek into the lives of the working class of the city. Shot largely on location in Santa Monica, the film reverses the focus of *Gun Crazy* and becomes entirely about money. There is ordinary lust, of course, as Brady falls for the femme fatale of the piece, Vera (Jeanne Cagney). There is even a wholesome love interest as the faithful ex-girlfriend/good girl, Helen (Barbara Bates), stands by her man and eventually helps in his final redemption. But ultimately this noir gem is about the postwar consumer society and what it does to those on the fringes of it.

The characters are all working-class poor, eking out a living in small, dingy apartments not far from the Santa Monica pier. They work in low-paying jobs in the same city, and they spend their free evenings at the Pier and along the Venice Boardwalk playing the arcade games, riding the attractions, and watching movies at the Dome Theater (long demolished). When *Quicksand* was made, this area was a working-class playground, not primarily a spot for tourists as it has become in the last two decades. Numerous scenes in this movie are set in this escapist world of amusement and entertainment in order to give the audience a sense of how the working class played. But for most working people, amusement ends after a single night of cheap fun and games. And these characters are no different. When their night ends they start worrying about money and the consumer products they cannot afford but constantly see all around them: nice cars, expensive clothes, houses in the hills above the ocean.

As with *Mildred Pierce*, whose fur cannot insulate her from the chill of murder committed by her own child, and like Mona in *Pitfall* modeling clothes beyond means, a garment becomes a metaphor. On their first date Vera shows Brady a fur coat in the window of a department store. As Vera sensually rhapsodizes about it, the camera remains on the image of the couple reflected in the window counterposed with a larger-than-life mannequin dressed in the fur. Her desire for that coat and Brady's desire to have enough money to take her out on a date drives the noir narrative down a deterministic road and through a series of events, aided and abetted by Nick, an arcade owner on the pier—played by the inimitable Peter Lorre, who blackmails Brady into committing a mugging. The film culminates as Brady is hunted for assault and robbery. The final chase through and under the pilings beneath the pier is classic noir, as the protagonist-turned-victim-of-events spirals out of control and tries to escape out to the sea and Mexico beyond.

In a Lonely Place (1950), directed by Nicholas Ray, was shot largely in the studio but several locations were modeled after actual buildings in Los

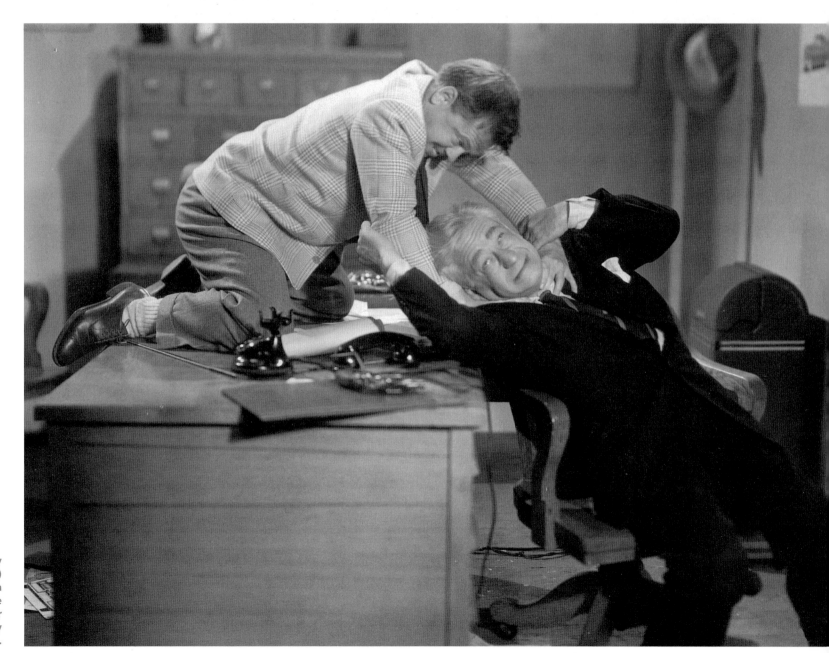

Dan Brady (Mickey Rooney) attacks his Santa Monica garage employer Oren Mackey (Art Smith).

Laurel Gray
(Gloria Grahame)
and Dixon Steele
(Humphrey
Bogart) visit
a nightclub
modeled on the
Garden of Allah.

Angeles. Giving the dysfunctional relationship between the protagonists in the film another, possibly more personal level of meaning, the Spanish style courtyard apartment complex where writer Dixon Steele (Humphrey Bogart) lives is designed to resemble the property where director Nicholas Ray shared an apartment with his wife, the female star Gloria Grahame (Laurel Grey), on North Harper Avenue in West Hollywood (not far incidentally from the apartment where a similarly dysfunctional couple—F. Scott

Fitzgerald and Sheila Graham—lived during the same period). The nightclub the alcoholic Steele often visits is based on the Garden of Allah on Sunset Boulevard, a nightspot which Ray and Grahame frequented.

In a Lonely Place is one of the most direct depictions of the repulsive syndrome of male violence in classic film noir and American cinema in general. As far back as Stroheim's *Greed* (1924) and up through *L.A. Confidential*, the depiction of men abusing women has been a hard sell for movie audiences. Ray and his

In A Lonely Place **courtyard apartments on which the film's apartments were modeled.**

screenwriter Andrew Solt analyze and criticize this phenomenon in an almost detached manner. By allowing the audience to believe that Steele may be a murderer for the majority of the film but at the same time using the iconic appeal of Bogart to create a sympathetic protagonist, the viewer is compelled to believe that violence, particularly directed against women, is imprinted in certain male psyches.

The centerpiece of this seeming contradiction is Steele's relationship with the smart and supportive, almost motherly, figure of his neighbor and eventual lover Laurel. She refuses to believe he murdered the hatcheck girl from the nightclub. She pulls him out of his chronic alcoholism and depression by her unstinting devotion. But inevitably she, too, begins to notice the potential of violence in Steele.

A key scene takes place on the beach off Pacific Coast Highway and Sunset Boulevard. Again, the coast represents an idyllic setting away from the noise and confusion of the urban jungle, and initially the scene is set up as such an idyll. They are happy, joking with another couple, until Steele finds out Laurel had been called into the police station for questioning and did not tell him. As palpably as Dr. Jekyll became Hyde, Steele changes shape emotionally if not physically. After verbally abusing Laurel, he races angrily along the coast, almost hitting another car and then beating up the occupant with scant provocation. After almost killing a stranger, Steele dismisses Laurel's

screams with a glib bit of bravado, "I've been in a hundred fights like that." Then he puts his arm around her neck using the same technique the murderer of the hatcheck girl had used to extinguish her life. Even after the final scene reveals that Steele is not the murderer, it no longer matters: whatever hope Laurel had for a loving relationship is irreparably ruptured.

The sense of speed and violence that underlies Steele's encounter with another motorist is at the core of *Kiss Me Deadly*. The adaptation of Mickey Spillane's novel by writer A.I. Bezzerides and Robert Aldrich relocates Mike Hammer from New York to Los Angeles. Like so many noir protagonists, the film Hammer (Ralph Meeker) is right at home in a landscape of somber streets and decaying houses. From Malibu to Beverly Hills to downtown, Hammer searches for "the great whatsit," a secret box that promises fortune. Like Hammer's sports cars designed for speed, the movie swerves frenziedly through a series of disconnected and cataclysmic scenes. As such, *Kiss Me Deadly* typifies the frenetic, post-Bomb L.A. of the Cold War era with all its malignant undercurrents. But this film noir also records the degenerative half-life of an unstable universe as it moves toward critical mass. When it reaches the fission point, the graphic threat of machine-gun bullets traced in the door of a house on Laurel Canyon in *The Big Sleep* in the mid-forties is explosively superseded in the mid-fifties as a beach cottage in Malibu becomes ground zero.

Lily Carver (Gaby Rodgers) about to burn after opening the "great whatsit" at the Malibu beach house.

Left: Lily Carver (Gaby Rodgers) burns.

Mike Hammer (Ralph Meeker) crawls away as Lily Carver (Gaby Rodgers) burns.

From the beginning, the movie is a true sensory explosion. In the pre-credit sequence, a woman (Cloris Leachman) dressed only in a trenchcoat stumbles out of the pitch darkness, while her breathing fills the soundtrack with amplified, staccato gasps. Blurred metallic shapes flash by without stopping. She positions herself in the center of the roadway, until oncoming headlights blind her with the harsh glare of their high beams. Brakes grab, tires scream across the asphalt, and a Jaguar spins off the highway in a swirl of dust. A close shot reveals Hammer behind the wheel;

over the sounds of her panting and a jazz piano on the car radio, the ignition grinds repeatedly as he tries to restart the engine. Finally, he snarls at the woman, "You almost wrecked my car! Well? Get in!"

The dark highway of the opening is a kind of narrative limbo: the elements of the plot have not yet been brought into line, let alone focused. At this point, *Kiss Me Deadly* has no clearly defined landscape to use as a textural reinforcement. The countryside and the rural gas station to which Hammer now drives are all unidentified settings. They are open, shadowy, and, even within the fringes of the station's neon lights, menacing. "A savage lyricism hurls us into a decomposing world ruled by perversity and brutality," writes Raymond Borde and Etienne Chaumeton in their original *Panorama of American Film Noir*, after which "Aldrich brings to bear the most radical of solutions: nuclear apocalypse."

For Spillane, Hammer's very name revealed all: a hard, heavy, unrelenting object pounding away mindlessly at social outcasts as if they were two-penny nails. In terms of attitude, the movie Hammer becomes a grinning predator, the antithesis of Chandler's urban knight and with survival instincts sharper even than Sam Spade's. Hammer is a quester. He is not an outsider in the noir underworld or any equivalent of a mythic "other world." If this is a foreign or alien milieu, Hammer is at home there. For him the dark streets and ramshackle buildings are a questing ground conspicuously detached from the commonplace.

Deception is the key to this world. Deception—not detection—is Hammer's trade. His livelihood depends on the divorce frame-up and the generally shady deal. For those on a quest in the world of L.A. noir, instability is the overriding factor and disjunction is the rule that the sensational elements in *Kiss Me Deadly* must follow. As the camera cranes down, the hiss of the hydraulic jack mixes with the screams of Nick (Nick Dennis), the mechanic crushed under the weight of a car. The pillar of fire that consumes the

Mike Hammer (Ralph Meeker) meets Friday (Marian Carr) at her brother Carl Evello's house in Beverly Hills.

The house on Doheny Road, which serves as the home of mobster Carl Evello, whose sister Hammer fondles in *Kiss Me Deadly*.

A wounded Hammer (Ralph Meeker) and Velda (Maxine Cooper) seek refuge in the surf (the ending long missing from *Kiss Me Deadly* until its restoration on video).

The apartment building on Wilshire Boulevard in Westwood, where Hammer lives in *Kiss Me Deadly*.

Pandora-like Lily Carver (Gaby Rodgers) on that beach in Malibu blends with the eerie growl of the black box that ignites her. Random acts—such as the simple "Pretty pow!" exclaimed by Nick as he jams a fist into his open palm—have no organizing principles. They transcend context to deliver a shock that is purely sensory. Still, they fit homogeneously into the generic fabric and the subversive whole of the narrative.

For years, a truncated version of the picture made it seem that Hammer and his girlfriend Velda (Maxine Cooper) perished with Dr. Soberin (Albert Dekker) and his accomplice Lily Carver in the beach house at Malibu. A recent restoration confirms that the severely wounded Hammer and Velda escape into the surf. But, as Aldrich himself points out, how safe are they cringing at the edge of a nuclear blast? In the final analysis, the "great whatsit" contained pure phlogiston. The quest for it becomes the quest for the cleansing, combustible element, for the spark of the purifying fire that reduced the nether world of *Kiss Me Deadly* to radioactive ash. What is actually in play in *Kiss Me Deadly* is not a standard archetype but a part of a process that Mike Davis describes as "that great anti-myth usually known as noir." Hammer is indeed an "anti-Galahad" in search of his "great whatsit." He and the city he traverses are perfect colloquialisms to stand in for and parody the Grail legend of Arthurian England.

Touch of Evil gives the viewer an idea of what

Hank Fallon (Orson Welles) looms large in a doorway at Tanya's place.

Tanya (Marlene Dietrich) meets Fallon in her house.

became of Abbot Kinney's dream by the end of the fifties. When looking for a Los Angeles location that could pass for Los Robles, a seedy Mexican border town, director Orson Welles was drawn immediately to Venice. By then the turn-of-the-century glory of this European-style beach town had faded, turned into decaying buildings and putrid waterways. Garbage replaced the gondolas in the canals, oil derricks dotted the once manicured landscape, and the Venice colonnade was badly in need of refurbishing. As the rich moved out, Venice's cheap rents created an oasis for artists, beatniks, druggies, and, in the sixties, hippies. Along with the free lifestyle and the countercultural revolution came a dramatic rise in crime, particularly drug-related. Hence, Venice was the perfect setting for Welles' noir tale of corruption and prejudice.

The much-discussed opening sequence, an unbroken craning and tracking night shot which lasts over three minutes, introduces the viewer to the derelict town as it follows a car with a bomb ticking in its trunk through the streets and culminates in a cut as the car explodes in a ball of fire. All around is classic border town. Rich Anglos like Linnekar, a corrupt real estate developer (like *Mildred Pierce*'s Monty Beragon), and driver of the car, bring their girlfriends here for furtive trysts. Latino thugs lurk in the shadows planning drug deals and planting bombs under the watchful eye of the pompous and slightly ridiculous Uncle Joe Grandi (Akim Tamiroff), whose toupee con-

Susan Vargas (Janet Leigh)
tries to flee a hotel in
fictional San Robles.

stantly slides around on his head. Honeymooners like Mexican cop Mike Vargas (Charlton Heston) and his Anglo wife Susan (Janet Leigh) seek an inexpensive get-away. The first 10 minutes of *Touch of Evil* economically introduce the audience to all these characters and to one more, American detective Hank Quinlan, who dominates the proceedings (he is shot most often in low angle) like the bloated and moldering older Charles Foster Kane Welles had created nearly two decades earlier.

As portrayed and photographed by Welles, Quinlan is the indisputable centerpiece of *Touch of Evil*. He is a detective with an unerring instinct who despises the denizens of Los Robles where he must investigate the "case of the exploding millionaire." His corruption mirrors the town's even as he rails against it. Quinlan manipulates the evidence to frame a suspect, who later turns out to be guilty. He forms an alliance with Uncle Joe, whom he later murders. He plants drugs on Vargas' wife and has her deposited in one of the decrepit local hotels to discredit the self-righteous Vargas, who is on to Quinlan's methods.

As he does all this, Quinlan eats candy bars, drinks himself into oblivion, and ignores the warnings

Oil Fields in Venice, California in the late 1950s, the location for the ending of *Touch of Evil*.

of his only friends: his assistant Detective Menzies (Joseph Calliea) and the fortune teller Tanya (Marlene Dietrich). Tanya's house, designed with a surrealistic touch, provides a sort of refuge for Quinlan until the final scenes. The slow chase through the canals of Venice demonstrates Welles' masterly use of physical location. Vargas follows a drunk Quinlan and his assistant Menzies through the polluted waterways, over the bridges, around derricks. Dark sky, water, and oil mix to create a disturbing, almost hellish backdrop. After Menzies, who has turned against his boss, shoots Quinlan, the detective's body floats out into the water like another piece of garbage. Tanya pronounces her friend's ambiguous epitaph, "He was some kind of man. What does it matter what you say about people?"

They Shoot Horses, Don't They? (1969) is an adaptation of one of the grimmest novels of the hard-boiled school written by Horace McCoy in 1935. To re-create McCoy's microcosm and its ambience of emotional disturbance and tawdry obsessiveness within the confines of a ballroom, the filmmakers used the French Renaissance motif of the 1924 La Monica Ballroom, although some interior scenes were shot at a dance club in downtown Los Angeles. The film opens with a view of Santa Monica beach, the same image of forlorn romance employed in *Mildred Pierce, Gun Crazy* and *Quicksand*. Against the same waves which washed across the title sequence in *Mildred Pierce* and the same pristine sand over which Huxley strolled and

Dan Brady fled, the young, handsome Robert (Michael Sarazzin), another tourist come to stay, gazes in awe at the ocean and the arcades beyond. The idyllic moment is short-lived. Like Nathaniel West in *Day of the Locust*, McCoy's vision as rendered by the filmmakers brutally rips the façade off the postcard scene to reveal the nightmare underworld of L.A. noir.

Once Robert wanders into the world of the ballroom and is enlisted by a depressed and bitter woman, Gloria (Jane Fonda), to be his partner in a dance marathon, the mood of the film shifts. Imprisoned in this building, unable to see the sun except in brief

Marathon Dancers Robert (Michael Sarrazin) and Gloria (Jane Fonda) in the La Monica Ballroom on the Santa Monica Pier.

The Santa Monica
pier and bay.

glimpses through a skylight or through an exit door blocked by thug-like "wardens," Robert is doomed. McCoy's thinly veiled existential metaphor of proletarian fate and the capitalist system entraps all the participants.

Inside the ballroom the promoters exploit their willing prisoners for the entertainment of the crowd, prodded on and manipulated by the deific promoter Rocky (Gig Young), and forced to represent various archetypes of the American Dream: girl-finds-boy; self-sacrificing pregnant mother; aging, plucky veteran; upcoming starlet. Victims of the Great Depression sweeping the country outside them, they dance for days on end and undergo humiliation for a grand prize of fifteen hundred dollars. The final scene, one of the few sequences like the opening set outside the ballroom, unfolds on the pier at night. The world is no longer bright and sunny. It is pure noir, so devoid of

hope that Robert acquiesces to Gloria's plea and puts her out of her misery. "Why?" he explains as the police arrive, "They shoot horses, don't they?"

Released midway between *They Shoot Horses, Don't They?* and *Chinatown*, *Hickey & Boggs* (1972) is a landmark neo-noir on several levels. By the mid-fifties the classic noir period was moving to a close. Externally, the enforced optimism of the Eisenhower era put postwar malaise in remission. By 1958 and the release of *Touch of Evil*, usually cited as the last major film noir of the cycle, noir had run its course. A few films with a noir-like vision such as *Cape Fear* (1962) or *Point Blank* (1967) appeared in the sixties, but there was no formal successor, no neo-noir genre. This changed with the release of movies like *Hickey & Boggs* in the early seventies. In *Dirty Harry* (1971), *The French Connection* (1971), *The Friend of Eddie Coyle* (1973), *The Outfit* (1974), *Hustle* (1975), *Night*

Moves (1975), and finally *Taxi Driver* (1976), a new, self-conscious noir mood was evoked by filmmakers, by both veterans of the classic period such as Don Siegel and Robert Aldrich and a new generation such as William Friedkin and Martin Scorsese.

Like many of the noir films made right after World War II, *Hickey & Boggs* was also shot on location with lightweight equipment owned by the producer Fouad Said. Heavily influenced by the European new wave with its emphasis on low-budget production in real, non-studio environments, producer Said and director/actor Robert Culp shot writer Walter Hill's reworking of noir themes and characters on a short schedule all around Los Angeles. The film focuses on the title characters, two private detectives (Robert Culp as Boggs and Bill Cosby as Hickey) compelled to face their own personal demons and mired in existential anguish.

Boggs is an alcoholic who is masochistically obsessed with his stripper ex-wife. Hickey struggles with a sense of futility and is unable to reconnect with his family. As they crisscross Los Angeles, they pass through a noir labyrinth of corruption, violence, and betrayal. As with *They Shoot Horses, Don't They?*, the film turns the conventional signifiers of the American Dream on their heads to reveal the American Nightmare beneath. Hickey meets his newest client, Rice, on the sunny Santa Monica beach as the decadent, effete and—as the audience might expect from

the noir tradition—thoroughly crooked lawyer lounges on the sand. In the background gleams the glaringly white complex of the California Club's beach facility, for decades an exclusive meeting place—no religious or ethnic minorities need apply—for the power elite of Los Angeles. Later they follow a lead to a cliffside mansion where a Black Power leader resides, staring out over the coast from a patio which has obviously collapsed into the cliffs below, symbolizing the place where the same American dream that drove Mildred Pierce has finally run out of steam, where the continent itself disappears into the sea.

In the course of a complex narrative centered

The beach club location for the meeting with Rice in *Hickey & Boggs.*

Al Hickey (Bill Cosby) and Frank Boggs (Robert Culp) in the final shootout at Point Dume.

on stolen syndicate money, Boggs is increasingly enfeebled. "I got to get a bigger gun," he remarks after a shoot-out, "I can't hit anything." The already disillusioned Hickey, who realizes that their job is an anachronism, which "is not about anything anymore," suffers the loss of his estranged wife. Much like the ending of *Kiss Me Deadly*, the unsettling and apocalyptic conclusion of *Hickey & Boggs* occurs in that same narrow strip described by Huxley between the breakers and the highway. Surrounded by surf and sand, the weary protagonists confront the thugs of the wealthy syndicate bosses who descend from the sky in helicop-

ters, automatic weapons blazing. Hickey and Boggs survive, but as they walk away from a scene littered with human bodies and mechanical wreckage Hickey restates his nihilistic judgment: "Nobody came. Nobody cares. It's still not about anything."

Altman's *The Long Goodbye*, another film in the vanguard of neo-noir, follows the geography of Chandler's novel and watches its post-modern Marlowe chase false leads from Hollywood to Malibu. Like Hickey and Boggs, Marlowe is now hopelessly dated, a chain-smoking, dark-suited forties' detective stuck in Los Angeles of the seventies. Unlike the 1969

Marlowe (Elliott Gould) visits Eileen Wade (Nina Van Pallandt) at her Malibu house.

adaptation of *The Little Sister*, in which James Garner portrayed the title character Marlowe and kept a retro office at the Bradbury Building downtown, the city of Altman's Marlowe, once a tribute to moderne/Spanish/ fantasy architecture, is now filled with utilitarian, high-rise, steel and glass buildings, epitomized in a visit to the 9000 building on the Sunset Strip. Even the markets have changed. The intimacy of Jerry's, where Neff and Phyllis furtively meet in *Double Indemnity*, is gone, and instead there is the impersonal all-night supermarket like the one on Franklin Avenue and La Brea Avenue (now called Jon's), where the perpetually

bewildered and disheveled Marlowe wanders the aisles late at night, looking for cat food while Muzak plays. The wealthy, who once lived in the manors of Doheny Place or Hancock Park, have left Los Angeles proper for guarded communities like the Malibu Colony, where Marlowe's newest clients guard their privacy.

The glass house on the beach, an actual location in Malibu, inhabited by the alcoholic writer Roger Wade (Sterling Hayden) and his long-suffering wife Eileen (Nina van Pallandt) epitomizes the soft, corrupt center the seventies' Marlowe discovers in his visit to the "paradise by the sea." There, Marlowe witnesses the abuse of Eileen by her husband, settings and events that recall both *Mildred Pierce* and *In a Lonely Place*. Visually the disheveled Marlowe's alienation from this new world is externalized at the Wade's party for their pretentiousness and fashionably attired rich friends. An uncomprehending Marlowe later in the film witnesses the indifference of this "community" of the wealthy as they peer curiously over the sand, tinkling liquor glasses in hand, at the scene of Wade's suicide by drowning. Finally, the link between all these worlds and traditional gangsterism is the violent, misogynistic Augustine (Mark Rydell), another abuser who interrogates Eileen about a missing cache of money.

But even in this world, Marlowe is still Marlowe. Again like Hickey and Boggs, his only defense against existential despair is to cling to his own idiosyncratic and anachronistic code of behavior. He despises betrayal and deception. Out of sheer doggedness, despite being beaten, arrested, and repeatedly menaced, Marlowe solves the mystery. Eventually he discovers that he, along with everyone else, has been set up by his friend Terry Lennox (Jim Bouton), whom he tracks down to a hideaway in Mexico. In an unexpected conclusion—not in the Chandler novel—he kills Lennox and leaves the scene, his spirits raised for the first time in the film. He has righted a wrong, eliminated a betrayer, and his personal code of honor is still

intact. More than that, with this final cold-blooded act, Marlowe momentarily sheds his anachronistic skin. No longer the knight-errant of Chandler's stories, and no longer discomfited, the neo-Marlowe becomes one with the violent times of a new era.

In *Farewell, My Lovely* (1975), another period film released the following year, the filmmakers take a different approach to re-creating the mood of the classic period. Adapted from Chandler's novel, previously filmed as *The Falcon Takes Over* (1942) and *Murder,*

The Argyle Hotel on Sunset Boulevard which acts as Amthor's brothel in *Farewell, My Lovely*.

My Sweet (1944), the film casts classic period icon Robert Mitchum as Philip Marlowe. At nearly sixty years old, much older and paunchier than the characters he portrayed from his classic films like *Out of the Past* and *Crossfire* (both 1947) through *The Racket and His Kind of Woman* (both 1951), older than Chandler's detective who was supposed to be 34 in the original, Mitchum still evokes the cynical yet idealistic Marlowe far different from Elliott Gould in *The Long Goodbye*, who cools his heels like a lost puppy in the Lincoln Heights Jail and whom the viewer would never suspect is capable of the murderous action of the film's ending.

More overtly than in the forties' noir films, much closer in tone to *Chinatown* than *The Long Goodbye*, *Farewell, My Lovely* deals with class structure in America and Los Angeles. As did Hammer, Marlowe has a grail quest. His search for Velma Valento, a woman who has become, ironically, Mrs. Helen *Grayle* (Charlotte Rampling), takes Marlowe from downtown on Central Avenue with its low-rent hotels and all-black nightclubs to the mansion (shot at the Harold Lloyd Estate) of the cuckolded industrialist Grayle (portrayed by hard-boiled writer Jim Thompson) and his promiscuous, duplicitous wife. Although he knows she is a spider woman, Marlowe forms an attachment for Mrs. Grayle, whose web of lies involves a phony "stolen" necklace and the unexpected twist of being Velma, the lost love of a hypertrophic ex-con named Moose Malloy (Jack O'Halloran).

The filmmakers retain much of Chandler's tersely poetic lines and hyperbolic metaphors as the narrative follows Marlowe around Los Angeles of the past where he encounters hostile and corrupt cops, a sadistic madam in whose brothel (the Argyle Hotel/former Sunset Tower Apartments on Sunset Boulevard) he is drugged and tortured for information, and ultimately the conniving femme fatale Mrs. Grayle. As did Chandler's character over the course of seven novels, this Marlowe survives it all.

The Sunset Strip, which stretches from Beverly Hills on the west to just past La Cienega Boulevard on the east, has long been associated with risky behavior, as speakeasies from the thirties gave way to skin clubs in the fifties and then edgy music venues, now epitomized by the Viper Room. Until it became part of the newly formed city of West Hollywood in 1984, the strip was legally a narrow stretch of Los Angeles County between the more conservative city of Los Angeles and the staid Beverly Hills. During the heyday of old Hollywood from the twenties through the fifties, famous nightclubs like The Garden of Allah and The Trocadero shared space with bordellos and clandestine gambling halls. In the sixties, as old Hollywood and the studio system faded and a new counterculture was born, the Strip became the center for drugs, sex, and rock and roll.

In the figurative shadow of the Chateau Marmont, The Classic Cat brought live nude girls to the strip. Gazzarri's and The Whiskey featured cutting-edge bands like The Doors, The Who, and The Byrds. It was to the Strip that young people from the south side or the valleys drove in to cruise, score drugs, and to party. Despite all attempts to crack down on the area, the hedonistic atmosphere continues unabated in the 21st century.

The Killing of a Chinese Bookie (1976), directed by the father of the modern independent American film, John Cassavetes, documents the Sunset Strip in transition. The days of The Trocadero and the Garden of Allah had disappeared and the energy of the counterculture sixties had dissipated as well. Clubs like Gazzarri's (now the Key Club), the location for the strip joint run by Cosmo Vitelli (Ben Gazzara) in the movie, were desperately trying to stay afloat. Cassavetes evokes this for the audience early in the film as Cosmo stands outside his club, surveying the half-empty streets, waiting for potential customers to tout. To Cosmo, his club is his life, a fantasy life as out of date as those of the detectives in *Hickey & Boggs* and *The Long Goodbye.*

In order to buffer himself from this reality, Cosmo surrounds himself with beautiful strippers, one of whom is his lover. He pays meticulous attention to all the details of the business, including the stage

show. To preserve his beloved club, Cosmo even borrows money from the mob, which he cannot repay. As a result they force him to perform a "favor" for them. And so the mobsters send him out to eliminate the Chinese bookie of the title.

Cosmo's obsession with his club will not even take a backseat to murder. On his way to the bookie's home, he stops to make a phone call in order to check up on how the show is going. Like Mildred Pierce or Dan Brady or dozens of other classic noir figures,

The dingy Key Club on Sunset Boulevard, formerly the site of Gazzarri's.

Morton (Seymour Cassel, far left) speaks with Rachel (Azizi Johari) while John (Morgan Woodward) has Cosmo (Ben Gazzara) sign an IOU backstage at Gazzarri's.

Cosmo wants to live the American dream in his own idiosyncratic way. He travels in a limousine surrounded by his dancers, takes them to Chinatown, spends money freely there or at local restaurants such as The Source (now renamed) and The Melting Pot (now gone), oblivious to future consequences. Cassavetes relies on his audience's familiarity with these noir precursors of Cosmo and thus exploits genre expectation to create dramatic tension. And so that there is no uncertainty, Cassavetes casts noir icon Timothy Carey, the grinning sniper in *The Killing* (1957) and petty crook in *Crime Wave* (1954), as his lead gangster.

Inevitably, Cosmo is shot by the mob. In the final scene he returns to his club, bleeding from the stomach, and becomes part of a show he has helped put together. The act is a tawdry cabaret piece reminiscent of the ones in *Blue Angel* and presided over by the Emil Jannings-like Mr. Sophistication (Meade Roberts) in white makeup and top hat. This figure is Cosmo's alter ego, for he too lives in an illusion, believing that he is talented when clearly he is not and that the bored strippers who surround him represent a world of sexual hauteur and refinement. Interrupting the performance, Cosmo delivers a somewhat rambling speech to the drunken audience who chiefly want to see the strippers disrobe. The fantasy dies hard in this two-bit entrepreneur, who like so many in the world of L.A. noir, came for the dream and stayed for the nightmare.

Cosmo (Ben Gazzara) is menaced by local hood Flo (Timothy Carey) in an alley near Gazzarri's.

The stage show featuring Mr. Sophistication (Meade Roberts).

3

Forget it, Jake. It's Chinatown.
WALSH in *Chinatown*

DOWNTOWN LOS ANGELES:

The Dream vs. the Nighmare

Visible remains and sites important in every period of Los Angeles' history are seen within a radius of a few blocks of the old Plaza . . . The business section of the city was formerly around the old Plaza, but it gradually expanded toward the southwest, and in time a new central district developed and left the Plaza region a backwash. This newer district, although still the focus of much of the commerce and gaiety of the metropolitan district, is already experiencing serious competition from the sections developing along main arteries and in the suburbs of the greater city.

Anonymous WPA writer in Los Angeles (1941)

The conventional wisdom is that Los Angeles has no real downtown, no center, no "soul" like other cities. Los Angeles, both city and county, is so expansive (over four thousand square miles) and fractured (including many other incorporated cities like Santa Monica, Culver City, West Hollywood, Beverly Hills, Pasadena, and Long Beach) that the mere concept of a center where commerce, entertainment, municipal, and residential life meet is beyond consideration.

As the above-quoted 1941 WPA publication on Los Angeles suggests, this was not always the case. Up until the post-World War II expansion of affordable housing to the suburbs of the South Bay, the Valleys, and the Pacific Coast, the city of Los Angeles did have a vital downtown with multi-ethnic housing in Bunker Hill, Boyle Heights, and Chavez Ravine. In addition, along Broadway and its satellite streets were a string of first-class movie palaces stretching a half-dozen blocks from Graumann's Million Dollar Theater to the

First Street between Alameda and San Pedro in Little Tokyo.

Current day Bunker Hill which was featured in *Criss Cross*, *M*, *Night Has a Thousand Eyes*, *Kiss Me Deadly*, and *Hickey & Boggs*.

Mayan. A plethora of successful nightspots and middle-class restaurants such as Clifton's Cafeteria operated in and around the central area alongside successful department store chains like Bullocks and the May Company. On weekdays Broadway was crowded with office workers and on weekends with shoppers and diners from the adjacent neighborhoods.

The city of Los Angeles itself was always a dream, a dream created by "boosters" (as Mike Davis calls them in *City of Quartz*) like General Otis, who founded the powerful *Los Angeles Times*, and his son-in-law Harry Chandler. They promoted Los Angeles as a new "city on the hill," a land of sunshine and unlimited opportunity. They advertised in newspapers throughout the country, supported regional promotions such as the Rose Parade, and enlisted other capitalists like insurance magnate Asa Call to invest in this new American enterprise cobbled together from the Spanish pueblo known as Our Lady Queen of the Angels.

In the process of building a major power center on the ruins of its Mexican predecessor (which are still visible in areas around the original Pueblo), Los Angeles began to experience a serious case of creeping rot. The dream began to corrode. For as the Otis-Chandler consortium saw their vision come to fruition, particularly with the growth of the movie industry, many of the first generation of Southern California entrepreneurs became even greedier for

The 1930's municipal headquarters of the Department of Water and Power, which figure in *Chinatown*.

wealth and power and less scrupulous about how to obtain them. The history of Los Angeles throughout the twenties, thirties, and early forties is one of rampant corruption. The rise and fall of Department of Water Chief William Mulholland, whose successful scheme to take water from the Owens Valley and pump it into developing areas like the San Fernando Valley was followed by the St. Francis dam disaster in 1928, is typical and among the most well-known largely because of the movie *Chinatown*.

A far more insidious instance of misuse of power in the thirties was the administration of Frank Shaw, the first mayor of a major city in American history to be recalled from office. Although initially opposed by the *Los Angeles Times*, Shaw appointed an Otis-Chandler crony as police chief, had the city buy a useless parcel of *Times*-owned land for many times its value, and followed the anti-labor union line of the newspaper. When Clifford Clinton, of cafeteria fame, organized an anti-graft crusade, private investigators were hired to dig out incriminating facts the police and press were ignoring. When Clinton published a list of hundreds of illegal enterprises involving gambling and prostitution that were protected by the police, the city sent health inspectors to shut down his cafeterias. When a car bomb nearly killed one investigator, Harry Raymond, the *Times* implied that Clinton had staged it as a publicity stunt.

Rail lines leading south out of Union Station in the 1980s. This location figures prominently in *This Gun for Hire*, *Night Has a Thousand Eyes*, and *To Live and Die in L.A.*

Ultimately a Los Angeles Police Department captain was convicted of the bombing. Presuming he acted with the consent of the city administrators, voters finally rose up and threw Shaw out of office in 1938, and the progressive Fletcher Bowron was elected against the wishes of the Otis-Chandler consortium. In 1950 Bowron appointed William Parker to reform the police department, which he did by turning it into a paramilitary organization (as portrayed in *L.A. Confidential*). Still, from the Sleepy Lagoon murder case and the resultant "zoot suit riots" of 1943 through the uprising in Watts in 1965, fair dealing for the city's ethnic minorities was rare.

Even as power shifted from reactionary fac-

tions to a more liberal coalition of Westside and South-Central politicians, the central city of Los Angeles continued its decline. The same group of developers posing as visionaries replaced rail lines with freeways and demolished residential areas to make way for business districts. Still viable neighborhoods like Bunker Hill, seen in numerous noir movies, and Chavez Ravine, which boasted low-cost housing, were leveled to build new split-level malls, expensive condominiums, and entertainment complexes like the Music Center and Dodger Stadium. Gradually, Los Angeles's downtown became soulless, a bifurcated non-center, which the majority of Los Angeles residents only visited to attend concerts or ball games. The now depressed Broadway

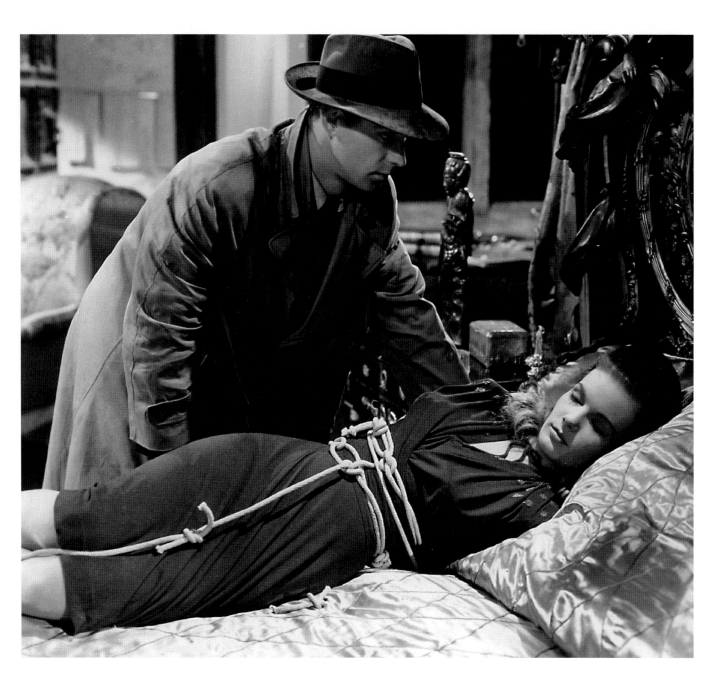

This Gun for Hire:
Hired killer Philip Raven
(Alan Ladd) rescues Ellen
Graham (Veronica Lake)
from Gates' house.

became largely the province of Latino immigrants who lived in nearby East Los Angeles and South Central.

Film noir begins its exposé of the downtown dream vs. the nightmare with *This Gun for Hire* (1942), co-written by Albert Maltz, renowned progressive and future member of the defiant Hollywood Ten who were jailed for refusing to testify before the House Un-American Activities Committee (HUAC). Entirely relocated from the greater London area in the original novel by Graham Greene, the film itself opens in San Francisco, where it establishes the character of its noir anti-hero, the "gun for hire" Philip Raven (Alan Ladd).

The audience first sees Raven in a boarding house, alienated and on the run. He is swathed in shadows (the film is photographed by John F. Seitz who would later shoot *Double Indemnity* and *Sunset Boulevard*) as he lies on his bed with a vacant look on his face. Immediately, the filmmakers establish the duality of his character with a visual shorthand which is both dynamic and economical. He hears his cat on the windowsill, fetches it some milk and pets it tenderly. While he is in the bathroom a maid enters and roughly swats the cat away. In response, Raven tears her dress and slaps her across the face. Within a few minutes the filmmakers convey the volatility of this early noir figure, the kindness that momentarily masks a killer.

After completing his latest job, the murder of a blackmailer, Raven discovers that he has been given marked bills by his employer Gates (Laird Cregar). He decides to follow Gates to Los Angeles and exact his revenge on Gates and his boss, the chemical magnate Brewster (Tully Marshall). He encounters Ellen Graham (Veronica Lake) on a train, ostensibly a performer but also a government agent attempting to infiltrate a ring of war profiteers in which Gates and Brewster are involved. Ellen also happens to be the girlfriend of Michael Crane (Robert Preston), the police detective pursuing Raven.

The assassin seems to form an inexplicable attachment to her, even falling asleep on her shoulder. Nonetheless, Raven is not so enamored that he refuses to use her as a shield to escape the police at Union Station and flee into the train yard behind. Raven, however, does not kill her, a sign—at least for this psychopath—that he does care, and Ellen continues her pursuit of Gates and his boss Brewster.

The filmmakers introduce the audience to Brewster in a telling long shot of a deco building in downtown, one of the few in that period. Inside the viewer sees a desiccated individual who recalls the wealthy General Sternwood from Chandler's *The Big Sleep*: " . . . in the wheelchair an old and obviously dying man watched with black eyes from which all fire had died long ago . . . The rest of the face was a leaden mask, with the bloodless lips and the sharp nose and the sunken temples and the outward turning earlobes of approaching dissolution." Brewster's voice is weak.

Hired killer Philip Raven (Alan Ladd) and Ellen Graham (Veronica Lake) hide in the railroad yards outside Union Station.

He cannot rise from his wheelchair. Although he exudes bitterness and decay, everyone around the industrialist is deferential, even the police who put more men on the Raven case on Brewster's orders, a reflection of the social reality: the close ties between the wealthy and the police in Los Angeles in 1942.

Ellen takes work at the Neptune Club, which Gates owns, a swank nightclub typical of those in the downtown area during its vibrant decades. After Gates becomes suspicious of Ellen and decides to kill her, Raven rescues her from Gates' Spanish colonial mansion in the East Hollywood Hills. Like the house in *Double Indemnity* two years later, a colonial revival location provides a contrast that mirrors the bifurcated social nature of Los Angeles. After trying to evade police through a gasworks, Raven and Ellen are again in the rail yard, crouching in the fog, as police searchlights scan the night.

While the couple hides out, Raven tells Ellen of the cycle of abuse he suffered as a child. However unsubtle, this exposition gives the audience the Freudian key to Raven's nature. Ellen, who represents the "good mother," binds his physical wound while she applies balm to his psychological wound as well with a chaste kiss. Enlisting him to help bring down Brewster and break the ring, she acts as a decoy when daybreak comes. Raven runs across the bridges spanning the train yards and manages to reach Brewster's offices where he forces a confession out of the dying man.

Raven is shot by the pursuing police, but dies redeemed, staring up at Ellen and asking, "Did I do all right for you?"

Coming as it does, early in the noir cycle, *This Gun for Hire* makes sophisticated use of the downtown geography and noir lighting style. The movement from Raven's surroundings in the opening to the decorative detail in the studio interiors of Brewster's office creates a visual equivalent for the social themes of Greene's original. The symbolic values of the train journey and the escapes through the rail yards also parallel the redemptive metaphor that Greene put into play.

John Farrow's *Night Has a Thousand Eyes* (1948, also photographed by Seitz) recruits similar images from downtown Los Angeles in a slightly different narrative context and effectively mixes, as did most of the films of the classic period, real locations with studio sets.

The movie begins in the Union Station rail yards at night, under the stars, where a distraught young woman, Jean Courtland (Gail Russell), considers suicide. She is pulled away from the tracks at the last moment by her fiancé Elliott (John Lund). She has been told by a seer, who had predicted her father's death, that she too is to die. Elliott and Jean confront the seer, John Triton (Edward G. Robinson), in a nearby café where he recounts his tragic story and how he came to be cursed with this ability to see the future.

While performing a sophisticated mind read-

Night Has a Thousand Eyes: Inside the Courtland mansion in the hills above Los Angeles, John Triton (Edward G. Robinson) examines himself for an "imaginary" wound.

Union Station was featured prominently in various pictures including *Criss Criss, D.O.A., Hickey & Boggs, Blade Runner,* and *Heat.*

ing act, Triton finds himself haunted by visions which come true, including the most disturbing one that his performing partner and fiancée Jenny, Jean's eventual mother, would die in childbirth. To prevent this, he abruptly leaves. Not knowing where Triton has gone, Jenny marries their former business manager, Whitney Courtland (Jerome Cowan). After he learns that Jenny does die when Jean is born, Triton returns to Los Angeles and lives on Bunker Hill, where the audience sees him trudging up and down to his dingy apartment while the Angel's Flight cars run up and down behind him.

When Triton has a premonition of the death of Courtland, he feels compelled to contact Jean. Before he can help he receives yet another vision which reveals Jean's own death. This fatalistic narrative retains the ironic twists typical of the novels of Cornell Woolrich and underscores them with the geography. The doomed Triton leaves Bunker Hill for the mansion of the Courtland family where he finds his own personal redemption.

T-Men (1947), directed by noir specialist Anthony Mann and photographed by the influential noir cinematographer John Alton, is shot extensively in downtown locations, again intermixed with re-creations of the locations in studio. In fact, *T-Men*, along with films such as *House on 92nd Street* (1945), *Call Northside 777* (1948), *Kiss of Death* (1947), *The Street with No Name* (1948) and *The Naked City* (1948), is largely responsible for creating a sub-category of the noir cycle, a sort of docu-noir. Influenced heavily by the neo-realist movement in Italy (*Rome, Open City, Bicycle Thief, Paisan*, etc.) and the street realism of still photographers such as Arthur "WeeGee" Fellig, these films often featured "behind-the-scenes" looks at the working of the FBI, or a local police department usually accompanied by an omniscient narrator.

Despite the presence of Mann and Alton, *T-Men* includes a tedious *de rigueur* prologue peopled with actual functionaries of the Treasury Department. Its realist credentials established, *T-Men* shifts to a series of night shots around Alameda Street in the industrial area of downtown where an informer for the government is pursued by a thug named Moxie (Charles McGraw) and brutally murdered in the shadows of several storage tanks. The audience then is treated to a low-angle shot of City Hall with its phallic tower and then a view of the Federal Building downtown near Union Station. Inside their offices, the Treasury agents discuss this new case of counterfeiting and the murder of the informant.

Two T-Men, O'Brien (Dennis O'Keefe) and his partner Genaro (Alfred Ryder), are sent undercover, first to infiltrate the Detroit mob and then its Los Angeles counterpart. The audience watches O'Brien arriving at Union Station and then walking a few blocks up the street to the Chung King Court in Chinatown, where he questions herbalists about a particular mixture that a suspect named Schemer (Wallace Ford) purchases. Following a lead to local steam baths, depicted in a hellish montage of diffused light and sweating suffering souls, he finally finds his prey at the Bimini Bathhouse (now gone) near Vermont Avenue and First Street.

One of Anthony Mann's most prominent themes in his movies is suffering and sacrifice, with a touch of masochism, evident in films from *Devil's Doorway* and *Border Incident* all the way up to and including *El Cid*. In *T-Men* Mann focuses on the long-suffering protagonists O'Brien and Genaro. In one scene O'Brien tails the elusive Schemer to a hotel in Santa Monica, which houses an illegal gambling operation. Here he purposely passes some counterfeit bills in order to establish his credibility with Schemer. As a consequence, however, the other players beat him brutally in a bathroom and throw him in an alley. As O'Brien rolls toward the camera, his face a mass of bruises, he smiles.

Later Moxie visits O'Brien's sleazy hotel room in downtown and tortures him physically, trying to determine if he is a real crook or just an agent. However, the most grueling suffering O'Brien endures is psychological. While walking through the Fairfax District's Farmer's Market, Schemer and Genaro meet two women who call Genaro by his real name. Schemer reports this to Moxie before his own "execution," being scalded to death in the very bathhouse that was his

escape from the dingy world all around. Moxie confronts Genaro and, with O'Brien watching, murders him. Mann remains on a close-up of O'Brien, the pain and helplessness registering even through the mask of the indifferent hood.

In *Shockproof* (1949), written by Samuel Fuller and directed by melodrama specialist Douglas Sirk, parole officer Griff Marat (Cornel Wilde) becomes involved with one of his charges, convicted murderer Jenny Marsh (Patricia Knight). Although depicted as a man of high ethics and morals, Griff becomes totally obsessed with this seductive and brooding "bad girl" almost immediately after interviewing her in his offices in the county building in downtown L.A. Like many noir protagonists, Griff has a sexually tinged messiah complex, which compels him to rescue and then possess this "fallen woman." Although she is unrepentant and continues to meet her lover, Griff coerces Jenny to move into his middle-class house on Bunker Hill and take care of his ailing mother.

Eventually, Griff's sincerity wins Jenny's affections. They marry secretly, again violating the ethics of his profession. The film soon becomes an example of *amour fou* when Jenny shoots her ex-lover accidentally and Griff abandons all his middle-class values and ambitions to escape with her. On the lam they eke out a living as day laborers until they find out that the man Jenny shot is only wounded and decide to return and face their fate. The movie, like much of Fuller's

Parole Officer Griff Marat (Cornel Wilde) interviews new charge Jenny Marsh (Patricia Knight) in the county office building downtown.

noir work as a director, has a strong sense of irony centered in its portrait of the initially moralistic and preachy Griff, who abandons his ideals for what seems, at least initially, to be simple sexual obsession.

Criss Cross, released the same year as *Shockproof* and directed by Robert Siodmak, intertwines *amour fou* and the criminal caper in the manner of *Gun Crazy.* The film opens on a slow, almost mournful aerial shot over downtown Los Angeles at night. Accompanied by Miklos Rozsa's evocative score,

the distant view of an anonymous urban landscape gradually becomes more focused as the plane flies down toward the parking lot of a nightclub. As the image dissolves from an omniscient perspective, this preordained movement inward, drawn by an unknown object or person, suggests a fateful undercurrent that pulls the camera in for a closer look.

In the parking lot, Rozsa's score cedes to dance music from inside the club and headlights sweep across the parked cars to reveal two lovers embracing passionately but furtively. The introduction of the protagonists exploits the noir conventions to plunge the viewer abruptly into their point of view and to isolate a moment that mixes fear of discovery with sexual excitement.

Steve Thompson (Burt Lancaster) and his ex-wife Anna (Yvonne De Carlo) are discussing their plan: after a robbery, they will double-cross Anna's current husband Slim Dundee (Dan Duryea) and meet at a hideout to the south of the city, in Palos Verdes overlooking the sea. Slim Dundee is the boss of a gang that is pulling off an armored car robbery with the help of a

trusted employee, Thompson. Economically, Siodmak sets the character's emotions: Anna, unhappy with the oppressive and possessive Dundee, yearning for the comfortable and safe; Thompson, obsessed with Anna despite numerous breakups and betrayals. In the next sequence, as an anxious Thompson drives the armored car en route to where his partners are waiting in ambush, he begins his first-person narration.

As his recollection begins, the viewers see Thompson returning to Los Angeles on the trolley below Bunker Hill. He walks to his family's middle-class house, which resembles the one in *Shockproof*, and is embraced by his loving family. But there is a restlessness in Thompson, something his family notices but tries to downplay. He cannot sit still. He nervously looks at the phone. He is searching for something or someone.

Thompson leaves the bosom of his family and heads downtown to a familiar club, from whose doorway the icon of City Hall looms like an ill omen. "From the start, it all went one way," Thompson laments in his flashback voiceover. "It was in the cards, or it was fate or a jinx, or whatever you want to call it." At the club suddenly there among the crowd is Anna, dancing with abandon to a band whose Latin rhythms complement her exotic beauty. She moves oneirically before him, as if

Present-day tunnel through Bunker Hill where Steve Thompson is dropped off in *Criss Cross*.

Anna (Yvonne De Carlo) and an anonymous patron (Tony Curtis) dance to the Esy Morales band in a downtown nightclub.

sprung from the depths of his overwhelming desire. Siodmak gives the audience a perspective that cannot literally be what Thompson sees—the foreshortened POV shot captured with a long lens belies that—but is rather a composite of what he sees distorted by what he feels.

This sequence is the key to *Criss Cross* and its doomed protagonists. The day-lit exteriors around Angel's Flight or outside Union Station or the full-lit shots inside his workplace or with Anna at the Bunker Hill flophouse the gang uses to plan the heist are all naturalistic in their lighting and composition. As informed by the first scenes, these sequences become functionally if not stylistically noir for, if Anna is not his, they all reflect Thompson's rekindled dissatisfaction with his environment. The expressionistic staging of the robbery with its violence, its dark masked figures moving apprehensively through frames filled with smoke from the robbers' tear gas canisters, creates a deadly excitement which is a nightmarish variant—again from Thompson's point of view—of the sexual promise of the opening.

More than Griff Marat or even Bart Tare in *Gun Crazy*, Steve Thompson is an archetypal noir "chump," a word his police detective friend uses to describe him. Like that other memorable "chump" in *Out of the Past*, Thompson will suffer any ignominy in

Left: Anna (Yvonne De Carlo) and Steve Thompson (Burt Lancaster) in the Bunker Hill flophouse where the heist is planned.

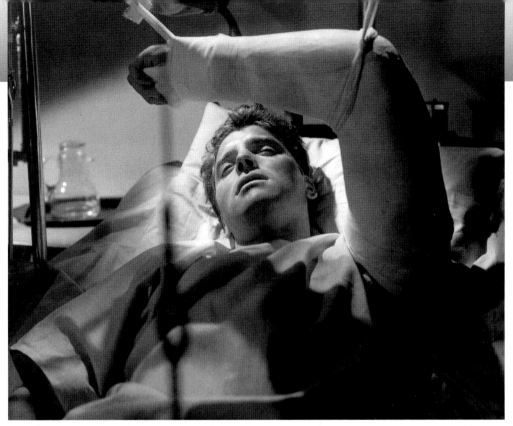

order to be with the object of his desire. In noir, mad love includes a masochistic dimension. Thompson's masochism will first land him in a hospital (the Kaiser Permanente Hospital on Sunset Boulevard and Vermont Avenue), painfully immobilized with his bullet-shattered arm in a cast and then, finally, dead with his arms around his lover.

Mad love first transforms Thompson from a law-abiding citizen to a criminal. In the hospital it drives him to desperation and paranoia, as knowing Dundee may come for revenge, he hopes simultaneously for and against Anna's arrival. In the last shot of the movie, the camera pans down at the beach house to reveal Thompson and Anna's bodies fallen together in a mortal repose undisturbed by the blare of approaching

A wounded Steve Thompson (Burt Lancaster) lies in traction in his hospital bed.

Kaiser Hospital in Hollywood where the injured Mike Hammer (*Kiss Me Deadly*) and Steve Thompson (*Criss Cross*) are taken.

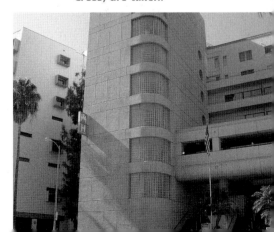

sirens, the inward sweep of the film's first shot, accompanied by Rozsa's same ominous music, is reversed.

Inspired by a German expressionist film, *Der Mann, Der Seinen Morder Sucht*, directed by Robert Siodmak in 1931, *D.O.A.* (1950), along with Edgar G. Ulmer's *Detour* (1946), is among the most existential of noir films. The director of *D.O.A.*, Rudolph Maté, was a cinematographer in Germany during the same period and presumably not daunted by the film's plot:

an absurdist labyrinth made up of coincidences and synchronicities in which an ordinary man, an accountant named Frank Bigelow (Edmond O'Brien), is fatally poisoned for signing the wrong document at the wrong time.

Bigelow tries to avoid his "propulsion toward death" (as existentialist Martin Heidegger defined "life") by accumulating as much personal experience as possible, which was Jean-Paul Sartre's own antidote

Chester (Neville Brand, left with gun in hand) menaces Frank Bigelow (Edmond O'Brien) in his downtown hotel room.

for the "nausea" of existence. But no matter how fast the character runs, first through the downtown of San Francisco and then to Los Angeles, he still ends as he begins: a "dead man walking" through the corridors of City Hall. The intricate, circular ironies of the movie bespeak a distorted and fatalistic view of the universe, where a man can report his own murder a few minutes before he actually dies

Bigelow is an everyman, or rather an *every-male*. Living in Banning, a small town east of Los Angeles, he finds himself hemmed in by his humdrum job as an accountant and frightened by the pressure from his secretary/girlfriend Paula (Pamela Britton) to settle down in a suburban house and raise a family, to become, like Forbes and his family in *Pitfall*, a proper consuming unit. But like Forbes, Bigelow is restless, as restless as any serviceman returning from the war trying to readjust to a life where danger is not a daily

The glass roof of the Bradbury Building in the 1980s, used as a location in such films as *D.O.A., M, Marlowe,* and *Blade Runner.*

occurrence and where the most exciting event is notarizing bills of sale.

While on vacation in San Francisco and staying at the swank St. Francis Hotel, Bigelow is surrounded by attractive young women brought in for a sales convention. After several flirtations he ends up in a jazz club on the wharf. There, he finds the excitement he is looking for: a beautiful stranger fondling him, bebop jazz played at a frenetic pace, a gallery of sweating, ecstatic faces watching in rapture. It is also there where a mysterious stranger in a scarf poisons his drink. After he is diagnosed with iridium poisoning, Bigelow tries to run from the diagnosis, frantically traversing the wharf area, returning to the scene of the crime. Denial and self-pity soon yield to a resolve to find his killer, and he heads for Los Angeles.

With the shift to L.A. comes a shift in his persona. Bigelow changes from a weak-willed malcontent to a "tough guy," the kind he might have seen in the Banning movie house. Now he manhandles women to get information. Now he steals a gun and brandishes it during a chase through a downtown warehouse. Now he is beaten up by a psychopathic thug, but gets his revenge by cleverly disabling his antagonist's car. The inevitable crash as they drive down Broadway, past

In a downtown parking garage, **Crime Boss Dan Langley (Luther Adler, center)** presides over the kangaroo court for child killer **Martin Harrow (David Wayne, kneeling at right)**, as fellow criminals **(including Raymond Burr, far left)** look on.

landmarks like the Orpheum Theater and Clifton's Cafeteria, becomes a liberating experience for Bigelow. He even finds the identity of the killer after sorting through clues more than Gordian in their complexity, and then shoots his murderer on the ornate steps of the Bradbury Building. Having compressed all this experience into his few remaining hours, Bigelow attains a sort of resignation that pre-figures Meursault in Camus' *The Stranger*. The frenetic pace of the movie crashes to a halt as Bigelow keels over, and the police captain pronounces him "dead on arrival."

It is remarkable that Joseph Losey's remake of *M*, Fritz Lang's 1931 German classic, could be realized in this country in 1951 at the height of the blacklist on which Losey, many of the actors (Karen Morley and Howard Da Silva most notably), and screenwriter Waldo Salt were all inscribed. For *M* focused on a child molester and murderer, an unlikely main character for the puritanical, self-censoring Hollywood studios to depict. Consequently when *M* was released it was picketed by various religious and anti-Communist groups and was pulled after a short run.

M combines the working-class milieu of downtown L.A. and implied tensions between laborers and bosses with the dark lyricism typical of Losey's work from *The Lawless* (1950) to *The Servant* (1963). Much of the film is shot on Bunker Hill and its peripatetic Angel's Flight. Here, Losey gives us a glimpse into the life of the residents as they socialize at street fairs,

Child killer Martin Harrow (David Wayne) with his intended victim (Janine Perreau) flees his pursuers at the foot of Angel's Flight.

Left: Current day Angel's Flight (presently closed), which was featured in *Criss Cross, M, Night Has A Thousand Eyes,* and *Kiss Me Deadly.*

Right: Angel's Flight at Third and Hill Streets in the early 1900s. The observation tower was torn down in the thirties. (Compare with 100 years later on page 102.)

care for their families, and coalesce in fear as the "pied piper," who uses a flute to attract the little girls, takes another victim. But as did Fritz Lang in his own American noirs and his original 1931 *M*, Losey understands how irresistible impulse enmeshes a noir protagonist and presents child murderer Martin Harrow (David Wayne) without prejudice.

Visual shorthand explains the motives of M[artin] when he returns to his apartment after killing another child as the camera lingers on the various objects in the dimly lit room: the forbidding picture of his mother near his bed, the child's shoelaces tied to a lamp, the dolls, the perplexed look on the killer's face as he stares at himself in the shadowy mirror. Losey manages to create an empathy or at least understanding for M as he is pursued by a crazed crowd then trapped like an animal in the Bradbury Building by a consortium of street criminals. Dragged into an underground parking structure for a trial by his peers, Losey permits the character an extended speech in which he tries to explain himself as he sinks to the cement floor in despair and self-disgust.

M also deals peripherally with the corruption of the city itself. Like the administrators of the Frank Shaw era, the police chief (Howard Da Silva) is intimate with the criminal gangs that dominate the underground life of Los Angeles: gambling, prostitution, taxi services, etc. When the mayor pressures him for an arrest out of political necessity, the chief in turn

harasses the crime boss to force him to assist in the investigation. Of course, it is these criminals, not the police, who finally capture M and mete out their justice in a kangaroo court.

Hammer's quest in *Kiss Me Deadly* takes him from Calabasas, where he nearly runs over Christina, to Carver's hideout in Chinatown with side trips to Hollywood (the Athletic Club) and Beverly Hills (gangster Nick Evello's house on Doheny Road). While the "great whatsit" detonates on Westward Beach Road near Point Dume, most of the locations are downtown

Mike Hammer (Ralph Meeker, left) visits the Bunker Hill rooming house of Christina where the Old Mover (Silvio Minciotti, center) is at work for Mr. Super (James McCallian) and Mrs. Super (Jesslyn Fax).

and most of them are gone. Christina's and Trivago's apartments were in Bunker Hill, the latter adjacent to the Angel's Flight cable cars under which Hammer drives his Corvette when he comes to visit. Also gone are Nick's garage on Temple Street, Carver's place on North Spring Street, Diker's House in the 600 block of Sunset Boulevard, the Main Street Gym, and the Club Pigalle down Figueroa Street.

In *The Crimson Kimono*, writer-turned-director Samuel Fuller, who began his career as a reporter, applies his characteristic hard-hitting, tabloid journalistic style to this story of racism and the American melting pot in Los Angeles. After introducing all the main actors and technicians in a brief title sequence over the painting of a Japanese woman in a kimono, Fuller then reveals his most important character with a headline-like banner over a night shot of the city: "Los Angeles, Main Street, 8:00 PM." A blast of sleazy, raucous chords plays over the transition into the interior of a burlesque house on Main Street, one of many such establishments downtown during that period, all of which have disappeared as the city government has moved to reclaim the old bank district in the late eighties and nineties. On stage is a blonde, zaftig stripper named Sugar Torch (Gloria Pall). As she finishes her lackluster act and returns to her dressing room, she encounters a gunman. She runs out onto Main Street, still half-dressed, dodging cars as the assailant pursues her and fells her with one final bullet.

Assigned to investigate this murder by the L.A.P.D. are two of its best detectives, Charlie Bancroft (Glenn Corbett) and Joe Kojaku (James Shigeta). These two men are typical of a new generation of police officers, the officers created by Chief Parker and immortalized in *Dragnet*: incorruptible, straight talking, and disdainful of pejoratives like "cop." However, unlike Joe Friday, Bancroft and Kojaku are not just tough talk. Without a second thought, they beat a suspect called "Karate" (Fuji) in a pool hall in Little Tokyo. They are proud of their military background and defensive of the honor of the L.A.P.D. and nothing like the corrupt detectives of fiction from Chandler to James Ellroy. Unusually for 1959, they are also representative of the multi-ethnic complexion of Los Angeles itself. Although one is Nisei and the other Anglo, they had served together in the Korean War, joined the police force together, and now share an apartment like brothers.

Fuller underscores his "rainbow coalition" view of America and Los Angeles in particular in several key scenes. The first is Joe's visit to the Evergreen Cemetery at First Street and Brooklyn Avenue where many Japanese-American veterans of World War II are buried. There, Joe plans to interview his friend and mentor, Mr. Yoshinaga (Robert Okazaki), about a lead

Detectives Joe Kojaku (James Shigeta) and Charlie Bancroft (Glenn Corbett) beat and then interrogate suspect "Karate" Shuto (Fuji) in a downtown pool hall.

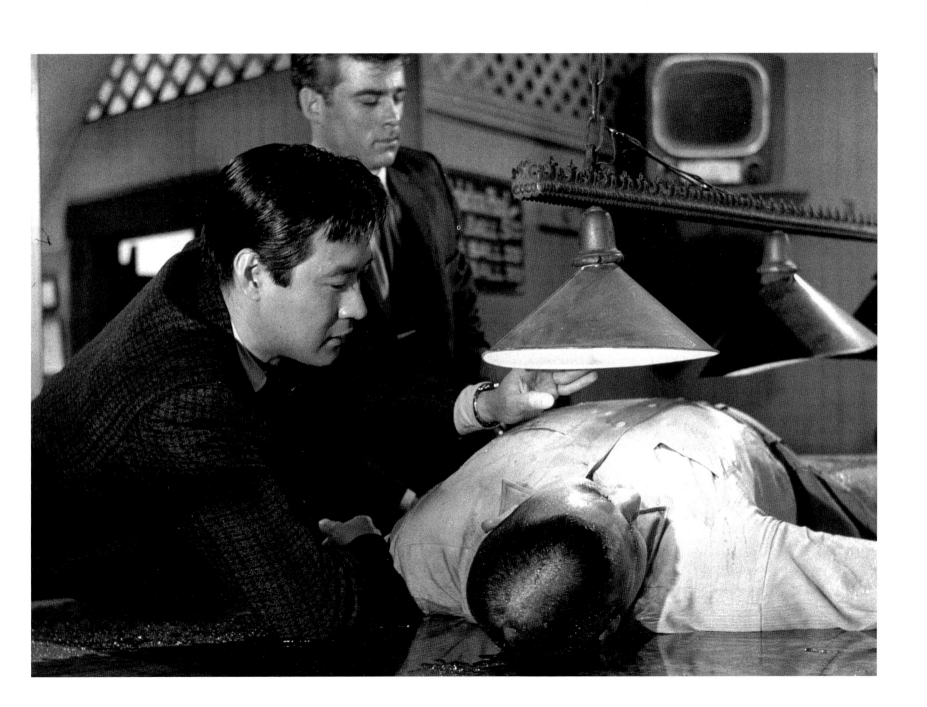

to the mysterious "Karate" who, with a man named Hansel (Neyle Morrow), was helping Sugar Torch develop a more sophisticated strip act, incorporating Japanese themes. But before this plot point is developed, Fuller focuses on the plaque in front of the cemetery, lauding the contribution of Japanese-American soldiers and uses an elegiac craning shot to reveal the graves of these men from an overhead angle.

The second and probably most important example of Fuller's positive, multi-cultural view of Los Angeles is the climax during the Nisei festival in Little

Evergreen Cemetery, oldest cemetery downtown and location featured in *Crimson Kimono* because of its many Japanese-American gravesites.

Samuel Fuller (center, facing camera) directs in downtown Little Tokyo.

Tokyo, where he presents the beauty of the Japanese-American celebration in which American marches played by a band of Japanese-American boy scouts mixes with traditional Japanese music to accompany the kimonoed and masked dancers. It is a celebration of two cultures merging with the spire of City Hall and the massive rectangle of Parker Center filling the background. It is also at this festival that the human story of latent racism and the physical as well as psychological melding of cultures comes to a climax and resolution.

Much more than a simple crime story about finding who killed Sugar Torch, *Crimson Kimono* is a love triangle between Anglo artist Chris (Victoria Shaw), who becomes involved in identifying the killer, and the two "brother" detectives. Chris is initially attracted to the brasher Charlie and his aggressive worldview, and he reciprocates her feeling. But after she is moved into the detectives' large downtown apartment to protect her from the killer who has made an attempt on her life, Chris finds herself falling for the more sensitive Joe, the son of an artist like her and a man who can converse about the meaning of art.

Initially Joe cannot handle competing sexually with his friend and tries to bury his feelings. In an unusual depiction of psychological displacement, one which a transgressive thinker like Fuller often favored, Joe turns his jealousy into a self-loathing racism, as he begins to believe both his friend and Chris despise him because of his Asian heritage. During a kendo match with Charlie, Joe loses control and beats his partner senseless, to the horror of the Japanese onlookers. Joe sinks into a depression, seeking advice from his mentor, and wandering the industrial area around Alameda Street at night, alone.

When Chris and Charlie confront Joe in a Little Tokyo restaurant, Charlie explains that what Joe saw in his face when he told him of his love for Chris was "normal" jealousy, not racism, and reminds

Gate to the main courtyard of Little Tokyo on First Street.

him that they share the same blood since a life-saving transfusion in Korea, making them "true brothers." In a final twist typical of Fuller, Joe remains unpersuaded until the confession of the real killer of Sugar Torch, Roma (Jaclynne Green).

After chasing Roma through the Nisei parade, Joe reaches the mortally wounded woman, who confides that she was wrong. Having killed Sugar because of an imagined affair with her own lover Hansel, Roma

has realized that it was "all in my mind." Fuller zooms in to a tight shot of Joe clutching the dead woman on a downtown street. Charlie grudgingly accepts Joe's apology but refuses to remain his partner. Joe rushes into Chris's arms and, in the middle of Little Tokyo, their embrace permits Fuller to use the city as a literal and figurative reflection of physical and cultural diversity united.

As effectively as Fuller, the filmmakers of

Left: Kimonoed dancers in the Nisei festival parade.

Right: Det. Charlie Bancroft (Glenn Corbett) pursues the killer through the festival crowd in downtown Little Tokyo.

Opposite: Detectives Joe Kojaku (James Shigeta) and Christine Downs (Victoria Shaw) rehearse the final scene of the movie in front of the crew.

Farewell, My Lovely and Hickey & Boggs move from the Westside and the Coast and utilize downtown L.A. to underscore character emotion. Farewell, My Lovely uses the Far East Café, a Chinese restaurant in Little Tokyo. The P.I. office of Hickey and Boggs in downtown is minimalist, almost depressingly so. The lighting like most of the film is high-key, almost glaring and unpleasant in a documentary style. The same is true of the bar the alcoholic Boggs (Robert Culp) hangs out in and the strip club where he masochistically watches his ex-wife's lascivious performance for a crowd of face-less patrons. The sun always seems to be shining brightly under a cloudless sky and through grimy win-

dows into cluttered and unkempt interiors. It is the type of weather—"eternal sunshine"—easterners left their homes for, but by the seventies the sunshine is tinged with smog, and filtered through some of the dirtiest air in the nation.

The filmmakers of Hickey & Boggs also make effective and dramatic use of public space in the movie, setting many of their action sequences in known sports landmarks like the Los Angeles Coliseum and Dodger Stadium. But on a weekday these venues are deserted, as if Los Angeles has become a wasteland where no one leaves their air-conditioned offices and homes. Cars are blown up, bullets fly, and illegal money exchanged amid the empty rows of stadium seats in the Olympic Coliseum. The anonymous meeting place of the mobsters suggests that they could be lurking in any of the office buildings downtown, a disquieting thought,

Left: Frank Boggs (Robert Culp) in his rundown office near Main Street.

Right: Face of Los Angeles Memorial Coliseum featured in Hickey & Boggs.

Left: The long-closed Los Angeles City Jail in Lincoln Heights, where persons arrested or released downtown, such as Marlowe in *The Long Goodbye*, Quemando in *Hickey & Boggs*, and Easy Rawlins in *Devil in a Blue Dress* were processed.

Right: A disheveled Marlowe (Elliott Gould) in the hallway of the Lincoln Heights jail.

much like the similar effect of using the 9000 building on Sunset in *The Long Goodbye*. In addition, the jails in that picture, *Hickey & Boggs*, and many other noir films are full of sound and fury, disorienting and disquieting, often set in the Lincoln Heights jail, which was the county drunk tank until its closing several decades ago. The 1953 downtown precinct and jail in *L.A. Confidential* is a seedy composite.

Chinatown, directed by Roman Polanski from Robert Towne's script, is certainly the best known early neo-noir, largely because of its critical and financial success. Equally significant, *Chinatown* is the first period Hollywood movie with a plot based on the history of corrupt politics in Los Angeles. Although, as Thom Andersen points out, the film obfuscates some facts, particularly by turning Mulwray (Darrell Zwerling)—the character based on Mulholland—into a tragic figure, *Chinatown* is set in the era of Mayor Frank Shaw, when the forces of darkness and corruption were firmly in control. "Of course I'm respectable.

I'm old," wealthy developer Noah Cross (John Huston) tells private detective Jake Gittes (Jack Nicholson), "Politicians, ugly buildings, and whores all get respectable if they last long enough."

Readers of Nathaniel West or Horace McCoy or Chandler's stories already realize that the "city of angels" in the thirties was not a pretty place. Just as the protagonists of *Hickey & Boggs* must confront the reality that their profession is out-of-date, by evoking realist fiction and the classic period of noir, by its very title *Chinatown* is a self-conscious reflection on the landscape of the era. To re-create this past, the film-makers began with many actual locations: the Bradbury Building where Jake's office is located;

Chinatown where the climax takes place; Lake Hollywood acting as a fictional reservoir which is being drained to convince L.A. residents that there is a drought; the house of Katherine Mulwray (Belinda Palmer) on Canyon Drive in Hollywood; the Eastern Star Home in Brentwood, whose aged residents are being used as shills on deeds to San Fernando Valley land; the Windsor in downtown standing for the Brown Derby where detective Gittes and Evelyn Mulwray first become sexually attracted to each other. Existing sites also provided the template for production designer Richard Sylbert's studio sets: the hearing room of the Department of Water and Power; the Hall of Records, where Jake finds more evidence concerning the water-land scheme; and the interior of the Mulwray mansion in Pasadena. This iconic inscription of an era that is actually pre-noir, coupled with muted color cinematography, often at night, permits an easy suspension of disbelief in evoking the period of Chandler, Hammett, and Cain.

Protagonist Gittes is also a pastiche of hard-boiled detectives Sam Spade and Philip Marlowe, although he maintains a successful enterprise by specializing in divorce cases, which Marlowe always disdained. He keeps a small staff in his office and is always scrupulous about telling his clients to try to reconcile before they take the step of hiring him. He

Jake Gittes (Jack Nicholson) photographs the apartment courtyard where Mulwray meets Katherine.

Noah Cross (John Huston) is restrained by a police detective.

Side entrance of
the Biltmore Hotel
where Evelyn
Mulwray drives off
after her lunch
meeting with
Gittes in
Chinatown.

even forgives the debt of struggling working class folks like Curly (Burt Young).

Gittes is intent on maintaining his dignity, even when snooping from the precarious rooftop of an apartment house in Echo Park, snapping pictures for his newest employer, the phony "Mrs. Mulwray" (Diane Ladd) of city executive Mulwray and his young "girlfriend," later revealed to be Katherine, Evelyn Mulwray's daughter. When those photographs are published in the paper, Gittes defends himself vehemently when accused of being a "cheap snoop." In fact, it is this sense of offended pride and not wanting to be perceived as a "joke" that compels Jake to continue investigating the case.

Like many noir heroes of the classic period, Gittes carries the burden of the past on his shoulders. The obvious symbol of this oppressive past is Chinatown itself, an underworld where Jake's efforts come to naught, where darkness and corruption triumph easily, almost off-handedly, in the heart of Los

Angeles, an enclave also symbolic of America's racist treatment of minorities. At one point Gittes tells the real Evelyn Mulwray (Faye Dunaway), as he lies in bed with her, sketchy details about the trauma that led him to leave the police force and cut himself off from emotional involvements of any kind. It involved a woman—"Cherchez la femme" Evelyn mocks—and his inability to save her.

Like Griff in *Shockproof*, Gittes is self-righteous, with a borderline messiah complex that makes him obsessive. For the viewer whose expectations are primed by the characterizations from the classic period, Jake's comeuppance is inevitable. Far from being purged, Gittes' demons watch as he becomes involved emotionally with Evelyn Mulwray, a woman with her own dark burdens including an incestuous relationship with her father, Noah Cross, and a daughter, Katherine, from that union. As much a quester as Hammer, Gittes also suffers as many physical assaults as Hammer, being beaten several times by a corrupt ex-sheriff and slashed by a Cross minion (played by director Polanski).

The old, therefore "respectable" Noah Cross is, in fact, the prototype of evil in the film. The very sound of his name alone invokes Pacific Mutual's Asa Call, a key figure in the 1934 campaign to discredit gubernatorial candidate Upton Sinclair and his End Poverty in

Evelyn Mulwray (Faye Dunaway) shoots at Noah Cross while her daughter Katherine (Belinda Palmer) looks on.

The commercial courtyard in central Chinatown used as a location in _T-Men, Chinatown, The Killing of A Chinese Bookie,_ and _Heat_.

California movement. Towne was fully aware of the key names in the history of Los Angeles such as Call, and the dirty tricks of an era when studio bosses at Metro-Goldwyn-Mayer helped anti-EPIC forces by producing fake newsreels in which unsavory-looking actors performed as Sinclair supporters. The primary history in _Chinatown_'s plot, of course, is the collusion between Mulholland and Los Angeles Mayer Fred Eaton as part of a syndicate that bought up large tracts in the arid San Fernando Valley and reaped huge profits when the aqueduct brought water from the Owens Valley.

Chinatown reflects director Polanski's innate sense of what political theorist Hannah Arendt called "the banality of evil," as evidenced in his diverse films from the early horror projects _Repulsion_ (1965) and _Rosemary's Baby_ (1968) to the overt _polit-werk_ of _Death and the Maiden_ (1995) and _The Pianist_ (2002). In order to achieve this Polanski focuses on the performance of Cross, whose stopped, self-possessed hauteur and gravelly inflection dominates his scenes. Cross believes he is right, even after Gittes confronts him with his incestuous behavior and the murder of Mulwray, his friend and partner. Cross' only response is that, given the right circumstances, people are "capable of anything."

The climax of the movie was at Polanski's insistence, as Paramount wanted a more upbeat finale with Evelyn and Katherine actually escaping the predatory Cross who now wants possession of the girl. The deadly ending, shot on North Broadway in Chinatown at night, is a grim evocation of the power of the noir underworld. The crowds, the wet streets, the neon lights of the Chung King Court—all create a sense of confusion and foreboding. As Gittes futilely tries to reason with his former colleague, Lieutenant Escobar (Perry Lopez), to arrest Cross for his crimes and permit Evelyn's escape, personal events that parallel real events of the thirties play out. Compliant cops side with the wealthy and powerful. Evelyn ends up dead and Katherine in Cross' clutches. The numb Gittes is left with no consolation, only the whispered warning of his assistant Walsh (Joe Mantell): "Forget it, Jake. It's Chinatown."

The next generation of neo-noir detectives also haunt downtown. For the rogue cops in *The Driver* (1978) and *To Live and Die in L.A.* (1985) downtown is still a good place to rough up the recalcitrant. Hammer drew information from Carmen Trivago (Fortunio Bonanova) by breaking a prized disc from his record collection. The nameless Detective (Bruce Dern) in *The Driver* and Secret Service Agents Chance (William L. Petersen) and Vukovich (John Pankow) in *To Live and Die in L.A.* are less subtle and, consequently, less menacing than Hammer. *The Driver* was directed by Walter Hill, the screenwriter of *Hickey & Boggs*, and revisits the themes of professionalism on both sides of the law. The focus in this film is on the specialist of the title (Ryan O'Neal), who handles getaway cars for a

fee; his antagonists are the detective and the neo-noir femme fatale, a foreign-accented gambler portrayed by Isabelle Adjani. In particular, the night in the cold concrete canyons offers an opportunity for a self-conscious, stylistic evocation of classic period noir, where an event as simple as a call from a phone booth becomes a complex metaphor: a man trapped in cycle of violence, under scrutiny from the police, surrounded by a figurative darkness as black as the night that surrounds him and underscores his isolation in the glare of the booth light.

Blade Runner (1982) is a dystopian vision of the future of Los Angeles. Based on the book *Do Androids Dream of Electric Sheep?* by seer/science fiction writer Philip K. Dick, the year is 2019, and Los Angeles is a city of polluted rain and perennial dusk, far removed from the "land of sunshine and flowers." The streets are crowded with a listless population overwhelmed by the darkness and corruption, all looking for a way "to score" or to leave the planet. Most of the upper class has already deserted earth for colonies in space where "replicants," artificial humans, serve as slaves.

Blade Runner's central city is a mix of location and studio, including the Warner Brothers "New York Street" (where Tom Powers was gunned down in *The Public Enemy*–1931), standing in for a futuristic Broadway. It is here that Deckard (Harrison Ford), a "blade runner" who pursues rebellious replicants, gets a lead on a group of particularly violent renegades, led

Agents Vukovich (John Pankow, center) and Chance (William Petersen, right) shake down a fence (Michael Chong) in the downtown rail yards in *To Live and Die in LA.*

by the charismatic Roy Batty (Rutger Hauer). These replicants have revolted on another planet and returned to earth to seek their maker, Eldon Tyrell (Joe Turkel). In the original release, Deckard narrates the movie in a laconic noir style and agrees to track down Batty under duress. From a meeting with his superiors at the L.A.P.D. headquarters of the future,

shot inside the deco Union Station, Deckard follows several leads to Chinatown, which is now a neon-lit swamp of water, steam, and human excess, overseen by electronic corporate billboards floating above the denizens' heads and advertising products and vacations none of these people can afford.

In his quest to identify more replicants and

Rick Deckard (Harrison Ford) searching for replicants in downtown L.A. (shot on New York street at Warner Bros.).

Rick Deckard (Harrison Ford) in the rooftop pursuit with Roy Batty.

"retire" them, he encounters Rachael (Sean Young), a retro femme fatale with a pompadour hairstyle and padded shoulders right out of *Mildred Pierce*. One of the themes of *Blade Runner* which mirrors the existential sub-texts of the classic period is the discourse about what it means to be "human." Deckard determines with an ocular scan that Rachael, too, is a replicant; but her highly developed brain will not permit her to believe she is artificially created despite what Deckard tells her. For part of the problem with this new generation of replicants is that they are achieving "sentience," an awareness of themselves as individuals, a sort of I-think-therefore-I-am humanity. The slave revolts on other planets are only a crime from the point of view of the masters, which even the emotionally detached Deckard understands. In his retreat, a luxurious apartment surrounded by cold block walls with Aztec-Mayan designs, a set based on the Los Angeles Ennis-Brown house designed by Frank Lloyd Wright, Deckard ponders the new type of replicant, whom he is assigned to "murder."

The film shifts its focus very suddenly with the appearance of the ostensible antagonist, Roy Batty, who in many ways becomes the noir protagonist of the second half. He is searching for his creator, exactly like the manufactured being in Mary Shelley's

Rick Deckard (Harrison Ford) and Roy Batty (Rutger Hauer) outside the Bradbury Building.

The elevator of the Bradbury Building in the 1980s, used as a location in such films as *D.O.A.*, *M*, *Marlowe*, and *Blade Runner*.

Frankenstein. His existential anguish is the same as Bigelow's in *D.O.A.*: he knows he is programmed to die and wants to know why. Like Bigelow before him, Roy seeks an answer within the confines of the marble and iron-grated Bradbury Building, where his punk lover, Pris (Daryl Hannah), seduces the lonely genius who lives there, Sebastian (William Sanderson), a creator of replicants. That trail leads to Tyrell, who has no answers. When his "father" cannot give him the information he wants, Roy crushes the skull of his corporate killer as casually as Bigelow shot his.

Deckard tracks Roy to the Bradbury Building and an ultimate confrontation on the roof. During the final scenes, the filmmakers associate Roy with religious symbols which give him an almost angelic quality: he drives a nail into his own hand, he speaks of fallen angels, invoking Milton's Paradise Lost as well as mystic poet William Blake, and a dove becomes his familiar.

But the most obvious religious reference comes out of the act of mercy he performs at the end of the movie. He saves his persecutor, Deckard, by lifting him up from the edge of the roof before he falls to his death. Roy then quietly escapes this tormented life as his systems shut down, inspiring Deckard to act on his own instincts. He goes back to his apartment, retrieves

Easy Rawlins (Denzel Washington) in his South Central neighborhood.

noir novelists, Walter Mosley. It is one of the few neo-noir films to deal directly with the unmitigated racism in Los Angeles during the forties and fifties.

A large African-American population migrated to L.A. during the Second World War to take jobs in the armament factories concentrated in Southern California. Consequently, ordinances were passed in various municipalities throughout the county and covenants written into deeds, bank mortgages, and leases which specified neighborhoods closed to "people of color." As a result of this "red-lining," African-Americans were confined to traditional "colored" neighborhoods, most notably the area running south from central Los Angeles between the Harbor and Long Beach freeways, which includes the Watts neighborhood and independent cities such as Compton. With steady incomes from the war industries, African-Americans built up these areas with middle-class housing, shops, and entertainment districts like Central Avenue which became a mecca for jazz musicians from around the country.

Carl Franklin's film of *Devil in a Blue Dress* opens near Central and 24th Street, with a detailed re-creation of the mood and style of the street: murals, movie theaters, bars, jazz riffs emanating from radios, and middle-class African-Americans on the streets. "Easy" Rawlins (Denzel Washington) has been recently laid off from his manufacturing job and is desperate to make his mortgage payments on his middle-class house

Rachael, and leaves this city of eternal night for the green hills and sunshine of undeveloped land.

While there were many other neo-noir pictures in the eighties, many were situated outside Los Angeles or shot in L.A. as if it were some anonymous metropolis. Three prototypical films of the last ten years revisit Los Angeles as period, contemporary, and "foreign" terrain. *Devil in a Blue Dress* (1995) is based on a novel by one of the best-known neo-hard-boiled around the Jefferson Park area in South Central.

The noirish plot engages as a thug named Albright (Tom Sizemore) approaches the desperate Rawlins and offers him work as a "detective," a job Rawlins rejects at first. Eventually his need for funds compels him to accept. The thug then sends him on a quest for Daphne Moret (Jennifer Beals), the missing fiancée of mayoral candidate Todd Carter (Terry Kinney), a scion of old money from Pasadena. A few scenes later, Rawlins visits Carter at his old world foundation, shot at the prestigious and exclusive Mayfield School in Pasadena. Carter's family connections tellingly parallel those of the Otis-Chandler family.

To find Daphne Monet, Rawlins must venture into all-White areas. On the Westside at the Malibu Pier, White punks from the Midwest harass him. At the Ambassador Hotel he must sneak in through the servant's entrance. It is at this swank L.A. landmark that Rawlins finds the mysterious Daphne, dressed in her signature blue. Like Marlowe's Mrs. Grayle or Hammer's "great whatsit" or Hammett/Spade's "stuff that dreams are made of," many are seeking Daphne. Carter wants her back because he is in love with her. Albright wants her for Carter's opponent, Matthew Terell (Maury Chaykin) because she has compromising photographs of Terell and young children. And Rawlins wants her so he can pay his mortgage.

In the process Rawlins is beaten by racist L.A.P.D. officers and almost murdered when Albright finds he is hiding Daphne. But the most significant element in the "metaphoric" nature of Daphne is her revelation to Rawlins that she is half-Black. While not as shocking as the revelation of incest in *Chinatown*, the overt symbolism of someone who is neither one nor the other underscores the artifice of rampant racism.

If Terell finds out that Daphne is Black, he could use it to destroy Carter, even though Carter has already withdrawn from the race out of fear of that discovery. Even when Rawlins kills Albright in a gun battle while rescuing Daphne from a cabin in Malibu Canyon (actually shot at the Disney Ranch in Newhall) and forces Terell to drop out of the race under threat of

Homes on 24th Street of the type used as Easy Rawlin's place in *Devil with a Blue Dress*.

Heat: **Lt. Vince Hannah (Al Pacino) in Chinatown.**

the photos going to the press, Carter still does not have the courage to "cross the color line," as Rawlins puts it. In a concluding scene shot at the Planetarium above Griffith Park, with a city not ready for racial mixing in the background, Rawlins watches Carter forego his love and spurn Daphne.

Heat (1995) is director Michael Mann's idiosyncratic view of Los Angeles. Mann's expressionism in works as diverse as *Thief, Manhunter,* and *The Last of*

the Mohicans situates characters within a frame and within a milieu that reflect the emotional arc of his narratives. The petty thief and FBI profiler of his earlier features are complex protagonists, whose stories play out in very particular landscapes. This paradigm reappears even in Mann's television work on the series *Miami Vice* and *Crime Story,* a long form narrative set in Chicago and Las Vegas of the sixties.

In *Heat*, Mann's Los Angeles is all neon, wet streets, and night, eerily resembling Ridley Scott's futuristic vision in *Blade Runner*. In one scene Neil McCauley (Robert De Niro), the criminal protagonist of the movie, after meeting a young artist named Eady (Amy Brenneman) at the Broadway Deli on the Santa Monica Promenade (she had first spied him at the nearby Hennessey and Ingall's Bookstore where she works) returns to her place above Sunset Boulevard. As they stare meditatively down at the city below, McCauley compares the "city of lights" to "iridescent algae," encapsulating Mann's own vision of Los Angeles in the film as an attractive yet potentially poisonous organism.

The danger inherent in the city becomes clear in the first scenes of the movie as McCauley arrives at Union Station at night to perform a daring heist of an armored car truck. As he and the members of his criminal crew gather at the rendezvous point off Venice Boulevard in downtown, under a series of freeway overpasses, they ram and then rob the truck, leaving all the guards dead. Hours later, at dusk, police Lt. Vincent Hanna (Al Pacino) arrives with his own crew to survey the damage and to begin his pursuit of the unknown killers.

The most expressionistic and explosive scene of the movie occurs in the bright light of L.A. sunshine, on the downtown streets around the Arco Plaza. As McCauley and his crew exit a bank they have just robbed, Hanna's team shows up to apprehend them.

What follows is a battle with automatic weapons through the busy downtown streets. Pedestrians scurry for cover, both police and criminals are shot to their death, and cars are riddled with bullets as Hanna pursues McCauley through the streets, only to lose him at the last moment after piling up a body count that would rival a Sergio Leone spaghetti western or a samurai film by Kurosawa.

The core of this movie, like most of Mann's

Collateral: **Hitman Vincent (Tom Cruise, left) and cab driver Max (Jamie Foxx) at a Koreatown gas station.**

films including the more recent *Collateral* (2004), remains male relationships. Both crews of police and of criminals are held together by the loyalty and dynamism of their leaders. The film utilizes the technique of doubling in numerous scenes to emphasize this point. Both crews have a celebration with their families at a restaurant: in McCauley's case, a place in Chinatown; in Hanna's at a more upscale American steak house. Both crews have personal problems which are dealt with by McCauley and Hanna. Both crews end up at the same locations in the movie as one shadows the other, including the Vincent Thomas Bridge at the L.A./Long Beach harbor where McCauley turns the tables on Vincent by taking pictures of him and his squad.

The central piece of doubling is that of the two protagonists. Not only are McCauley and Hanna played by the two most prestigious Italian-American actors of their generation, both with New York roots, but they are depicted as flawed in the same manner. Two scenes in the movie visually and verbally reinforce this doppelganger effect.

The first is when they meet in a restaurant, their only meeting before the resolution. Hanna is curious to see face-to-face the man who has stymied him at every junction. As they sit across from each other they are physically and emotionally matched. Both are consummate professionals who have sacrificed everything in their lives, including home and family. McCauley has no connections at all except Eady, who at this point is only a one-night stand; Hanna has gone through several marriages and his newest one is on the verge of collapse. They are also emotionally unavailable to others, especially women. They can both say "the words" and even show affection by their actions, but when it comes to a crisis they feel they have to be alone and live with their "angst," as Hanna calls it.

The second scene that solidifies the relationship between these two lonely and tormented protagonists is the ending on the runway at Los Angeles International Airport. Hanna has followed McCauley there in order to prevent him from boarding a chartered plane and escaping prosecution. In the ensuing gunfight, Hanna fatally wounds McCauley. As McCauley lies dying he stretches out his hand to the other man who grasps it. The final shot is a poignant one, almost homoerotic in context. The camera reveals the two men in silhouette, holding hands on the runway, as the white lights from the airport glare in the distance.

Mann's *Collateral* (2004) is an even more compressed and contained nightmare vision of downtown Los Angeles: a hit man hires a hapless cab driver to take him on his rounds. In a single night, Mann replicates aspects of many classic period quests, particularly Hammer's in *Kiss Me Deadly*, with scenes in dark alleys, gas stations, morgues, and jazz clubs.

Yamamoto (Takeshi Kitano) and his girlfriend Marina (Joy Nakagawa) outside his headquarters in downtown L.A. in *Brother.*

Often those on the outside are the most penetrating observers of the ethos of a city or country. This was true of Los Angeles in the classic period of noir where immigrants like Billy Wilder, Robert Siodmak, and Fritz Lang produced some of the darkest examples of L.A. noir. With *Brother* (2000), written and directed by the deconstructionist auteur Takeshi Kitano, a "tourist" noir is defined. A foreign director and star, who barely speaks the language, nonetheless constructs a trenchant vision of a Los Angeles at the edge of the 21st century. In fact, by 1990, a significant number of the black-glass corporate hotels and office buildings, a considerable portion of downtown real

estate, were controlled by Japanese companies. Outside these actual "Nakatomi" Towers, as the fictional high-rise of *Die Hard* (1988) is named, the downtown areas are peopled by immigrants from Latin America and Korea in a landscape very different from the noir era of fifty years ago.

Brother opens in the modernistic LAX as a contemplative Yamamoto (Kitano), a yakuza in exile from his home for being a loose cannon, waits for a taxi to take him to his brother. He finds clues to his brother's whereabouts in a Japanese restaurant on the Miracle Mile of Wilshire Boulevard. This lead takes him to the center of the city at Sixth Street and Main Street,

Left: Pacific Electric at 6th and Main Streets, used as a location in *L.A. Confidential* and *Brother*.

Right: Cole's, home of the P.E. Buffet restaurant in the Pacific Electric and inspiration for the fictional "Night Owl Cafe" across the street in *L.A. Confidential* and a dining spot in *Brother*.

where he is accosted by an African-American named Denny (Omar Epps) who tries to extort money from a man who seems like a rich helpless Japanese tourist. Yamamoto responds with an outburst of extreme violence, one of many in the movie. He picks up a broken bottle and gouges at the man's eye.

Yamamoto finds his brother (Claude Maki) holed up in the derelict landmark, the Pacific Electric Building at Sixth and Main. He is now a member of a multi-ethnic gang of drug dealers, which includes Denny, who does not remember Yamamoto because "all

Japanese look the same." Gradually Yamamoto grows to like this group of misfits and their depressed, industrial neighborhood because it reminds him of where he grew up. In long Zen-like scenes, typical of Kitano's work, the *yakuza* flies paper airplanes from the roof of the Pacific Electric Building, cheats at games with Denny, and stares at the Amtrak railroad yard in the distance while around him are the corporate high rises of the unseen executives, both Anglo and Japanese, who have no contact with his world of the streets.

Intercut with these alienated and contempla-

tive sequences are scenes of stylized, expressionistic violence, in the tradition of Japanese *yakuza* movies. Yamamoto and his multi-ethnic gang systematically defeat their counterparts, first the cholos and the African-Americans and then the Japanese mobsters of Little Tokyo, until the most powerful Japanese orabun or gang boss joins Yamamoto's "family."

But when Yamamoto and his "brothers" finally go up against the Italian Mafia, they are both outnumbered and outgunned. In an elegiac series of shootouts, Yamamoto's gang is eliminated. The exiled yakuza must watch helplessly as his girlfriend and his brother are cut down. In another strikingly violent scene under a bridge near Sixth Street, all the audience sees for most of the sequence are flashes of gunfire which illuminate the dead bodies. Convinced fatalistically that the end is near, the deadpan Yamamoto tells Denny, with whom he has formed a bond, to "run away" then immediately makes a joke of it when Denny reacts with shock.

The final scene of the movie takes place in Palmdale in the northern part of Los Angeles County, in a deserted motel and nearby diner. There, Yamamoto awaits his fate at the hands of the Mafia. He has sent Denny on his way out of the gang hell with a gym bag full of money and rescued at least one "brother" (the term is used very much as it was in its predecessor *Heat*) from the holocaust. As a line of limousines pull up outside, he gives the owner of the diner

some money to cover the impending damage and walks out into the desert sun in slow motion. The audience sees only a barrage of bullets as they shatter the red doors, in a scene which echoes the end of *The Big Sleep* and mirrors the fatalism and violence of fifties noir.

City Hall was featured with various degrees of prominence in numerous classic period noir including *T-Men, Shockproof, Crimson Kimono, Pitfall, Criss Cross* and most recently *L.A. Confidential.*

I turned north and swung over to Highland, out over Cahuenga Pass and down on to Ventura Boulevard, past Studio City and Sherman Oaks and Encino. There was nothing lonely about the trip. There never is on that road . . . Tired men in dusty coupes and sedans winced and tightened their grip on the wheel and ploughed on north and west towards home and dinner, an evening with the sports page, the blatting of the radio, the whining of their spoiled children and the gabble of their silly wives. I drove on past the gaudy neons and the false fronts behind them, the sleazy hamburger joints that look like palaces under the colors, the brilliant counters, and the sweaty greasy kitchens that would have poisoned a toad.

RAYMOND CHANDLER
The Little Sister

THE 'BURBS:

The Dream Re-Created?

The suburbs in Los Angeles City and County were created by an intimate partnership between industry and government on a local and national level. The oldest suburbs of Los Angeles were clustered around Pasadena to the north and prevented from significant expansion by the coastal range. As discussed earlier, the possibility of creating tracts for large numbers of single family homes to the west of Pasadena in the San Fernando Valley was made possible by Mulholland in 1913; but the process of development in the area was much slower than originally imagined. Such aptly named municipalities as "Studio City" and "North Hollywood," both part of Los Angeles city, developed first in the eastern end of the Valley adjacent to the Universal and Warner Bros. complexes and a short commute through the Cahuenga pass from Los Angeles and downtown. When Gittes visits the west Valley in *Chinatown* all he finds are orange groves and angry citrus farmers who shoot up his car.

After the Second World War the transient population of armament workers became part of a process for retooling "factories for peace," meaning production lines of cars, household appliances, and any other items consumers of the post-war era craved. The federal government sped up the process with low interest housing loans as part of its "G.I. Bill" and a new generation of

Jake Gittes (Jack Nicholson) visits
a San Fernando Valley orange grove.

developers pushed housing in the West Valley. Older commuter routes evolved into a grid of freeways, starting with the Arroyo Seco Parkway (now the quaint and antiquated Pasadena Freeway). By the end of the fifties, aerospace plants opened in what had been the Warner Movie Ranch at the western edge of the Valley. Test firings of rocket engines lit the night sky in the Santa Susana pass around where Cody Jarrett's gang had hijacked a train in *White Heat* (1949).

The San Gabriel Valley to the east of Pasadena was a slightly different case as were the South Bay and Long Beach areas west and east respectively of the city port in San Pedro. Both regions already had single-housing neighborhoods. Since their inceptions in the 19th entury, Pasadena and Glendale had been a center for Eastern old wealth and culture. They took pride in their designer mansions as well as their museums and libraries and looked with disdain at the working metropolis to the south. As postwar San Gabriel Valley experienced the same influx of veterans and their families, in and around Pasadena and Glendale, restrictive covenants began to become standard in their real estate deeds. The South Bay/Long Beach region, on the other hand, was always a working class area, with many of its residents employed by the harbor complex and other industries in that corridor such as petroleum, meatpacking, and construction material.

Unlike the San Fernando Valley, which was almost entirely annexed by the city of Los Angeles, San

Gabriel officially became part of the county of Los Angeles in the early part of the 20th century, but its municipal areas were independent cities or unincorporated communities separate from Los Angeles. Whether named or portrayed anonymously as the "Metropolitan Police," the L.A.P.D. is the prototype for law enforcement in the classic period of film noir and early television spin-offs such as *Dragnet*. Nonetheless, in the postwar era there were and are more than forty independent police forces in the county in addition to the sizeable Sheriff's Department.

Amid the tract houses, cheaply constructed and mind-numbingly similar in design, the shopping districts and malls soon became the hangouts of disaffected suburban teens who cruised in custom cars, those "fast boys in stripped-down Fords," as Chandler described them, who "shot in and out of the traffic streams, missing fenders by a sixteenth of an inch." Unlike the city proper, the Valley weather was more extreme. Frost menaced the citrus crop on winter nights, and every decade or so, snow briefly fell along the highways Marlowe drove past "fat straight rows of orange groves." Probably the most-quoted Chandler-ism is about the valley's Santa Ana winds, "those hot dry winds that come down through the mountain passes and curl your hair and make your nerves jump and your skin itch. On nights like that every booze party ends in a fight. Meek little wives feel the edge of the carving knife and study their hus-bands' necks. Anything can happen."

The corrosion of the dream in the suburbs was immediate. As Reaganomics took hold in the eighties and nineties, rust crept across abandoned factories. In the nineties as the majority of high-paying industrial jobs moved to third world countries, a globalized economy of multi-national cartels further polarized the class structure in Los Angeles. This hardening of class divisions was most apparent in the suburbs. Cheaply manufactured houses and apartments became dilapidated and a new wave of poor immigrants moved into the area, displacing the ensconced White working class. Gang-banging, drug trafficking, and production of pornography became new sources of income for these economically impacted areas. The menace became much more palpable than fast boys in Fords who narrowly missed your car.

San Fernando Valley orange groves in the 1980s.

Double Indemnity stages its suspenseful murder and deception scene at the Spanish colonial style Glendale Train Station, although Billy Wilder changed the sign to indicate that it was the Pasadena Station. In setting his movie's most sordid scene, the disposal of the victim's body, in these exclusive suburbs, Wilder and co-writer Chandler reaffirm that in a luxurious locale where even meek housewives can contemplate murder, femme fatales like Phyllis Dietrichson embrace it with gusto.

T-Men stages its climax at the L.A./Long Beach Harbor. It is a particularly tense and violent scene in which O'Brien is under suspicion for being a double agent and is brought before the top bosses of the crime ring to determine whether or not the counterfeit plates in his possession are recognizable. Although the mob's photographic expert eventually vouches for the plates, an agonized O'Brien, who has already witnessed the

Walter Neff (Fred MacMurry, center) and Phyllis Dietrichson (Barbara Stanwyck) dump the body of her husband on the track.

Glendale Train Station, used as the location for the night train trip in *Double Indemnity*: the front side.

killing of his partner Genaro, must wait to learn if he will be murdered too, not realizing that a group of government agents have been tipped off and are on their way to the ship to arrest the gang.

The police arrive and fire tear-gas into the freighter, which permits O'Brien to pursue Moxie throughout the ship, intent on wreaking revenge for the death of his partner. Although Moxie shoots him in the stomach, O'Brien unleashes a volley of bullets. With Moxie dead and the ring destroyed, the stentorian narrator hails O'Brien as a hero. The irony, of course, as the camera pans to a photo of O'Brien's murdered partner, in the same magazine which features O'Brien's "heroic" story, is that no palliative can revive the dead or remove the scars, that the noir underworld itself and its menace survive any individual triumph by the forces of law and order.

Criss Cross also concludes in the South Bay. The would-be refuge of Thompson and Anna is evoked by a few location shots around Palos Verdes, in the hills above the sea, mixed with studio interiors and matte shots. Prototypically classic period films use vistas of the mountains or ocean to symbolize escape from the troubled world of L.A. noir. Thompson's trip out to the armored car yard and over the bridge into the deadly ambush, however, all shot in the harbor area, is anything but tranquil and even Anna and Thompson's hideaway turns into a trap.

Anna has doublecrossed both her former and

Walter Neff (Fred MacMurry, center) and Phyllis Dietrichson (Barbara Stanwyck) return to her car after dumping the body of her husband on the track.

current husbands which becomes obvious to Thompson when he surprises her packing her bags, eager to escape with the money. She tells the stricken Steve, "You always have to look out for yourself." He responds, obsessed with her to the end, "I just wanted you." Dundee arrives with a flash of car headlights in the darkness. Anna runs to Steve's arms and Dundee pronounces the doomed lovers' epitaph, "She's all yours now."

Released the same year as *Criss Cross, White Heat,* directed by veteran Raoul Walsh, is fully embedded in suburban noir as it moves freely from one end of Los Angeles to the other. As noted, the film opens in the northwest part of the San Fernando Valley at the Southern Pacific Railroad tunnel in Chatsworth. Two different hideouts of the Cody Jarrett (James Cagney) gang are situated to the south in the Warner Ranch. In North Hollywood and Burbank, respectively, there is a motel in which the gang holes up in and the Sun Val Drive-In where Cody and his mother plan his escape from the police. And in the final scenes, tipped by undercover agent Hank Fallon (Edmond O'Brien, police track the criminals through downtown, past City Hall, south on Alameda Street to the South Bay

Top: Slim Dundee (Dan Duryea) corners Anna (Yvonne De Carlo) and Steve Thompson (Burt Lancaster) in their Palos Verdes hideout.

Bottom: Anna (Yvonne De Carlo) and Steve Thompson (Burt Lancaster) await their noir fate in their Palos Verdes hideout.

and the refinery at 198th Street and Figueroa Street.

The filmmakers establish the noir protagonist's twisted psychology early in the movie. At the robbery of the train, Cody guns down the engineer simply because the hapless man has heard his first name. At the gang's hideout, Jarrett sends one minion back to dispatch a wounded comrade, scalded in the heist and unable to move on with them. Jarrett is also oedipally obsessed with his mother, a Ma Barker-type. Even though he is married to the sensual Verna (Virginia Mayo), he alternately ignores her and physically abuses her, especially if she dares to criticize his mother (Margaret Wycherly) in any way.

Cody's tie to his possessive mother is like a sociopathic mental umbilical cord. While Jarrett is incarcerated in Illinois, where he had surrendered to a lesser charge in order to divert the authorities in Los Angeles from suspecting him for the murder of the train engineer, Fallon stands in for Jarrett's mother, even massaging the gang boss' brow as his mother did in order to quell his seizures. Consequently, Fallon becomes a "kid brother" in a relationship rife with homoerotic overtones.

When Cody learns that his mother is dead, killed by Verna in collusion with her new lover Big Ed (Steve Cochran), he throws a fit in the mess hall and is carried from the facility, screaming and crying like a small child. With his mother gone, the proxy relationship with Fallon becomes even more important, and Jarrett chooses to take this surrogate parent with him when he breaks out of prison. During the famous climax at the oil refinery, where Cody learns of Fallon's treachery, Cagney portrays Jarrett as enraged and bitter. The police interrupt the robbery and corner Jarrett atop a massive chemical storage tank. Realizing there is no way out, Jarrett fires into the tank and calls out maniacally to his mother, "Top of the world, Ma," as he is engulfed in flames.

Wilmington refineries and storage tanks featured in the climax of *White Heat.*

While much of *Farewell, My Lovely* was shot downtown at colorful locations such as the now-closed Far East Café in Little Tokyo, many scenes were in the 'burbs. The climax is in Long Beach at the pier where the Queen Mary sits. Marlowe first visits the area to meet Moose Malloy, although the arcade scene is actually shot at the Santa Monica Pier. Marlowe learns that Mrs. Grayle/Velma has connections with a sharpster named Brunette (Anthony Zerbe) who runs a high-stakes gambling ship, which is staged on the Queen Mary. Not realizing Malloy has followed him, Marlowe boards the vessel and confronts Brunette. Mrs. Grayle is also present, and it finally becomes apparent that she is Moose's faithless Velma. Moose is shot, but he manages to kill Velma before Marlowe can intercede. Unable to save Moose or even successfully complete his assignment, a chagrined Marlowe returns to the pier, disillusioned and slightly tarnished once again.

To Live and Die in LA also moves freely from central Los Angeles to its outskirts. The detective's beach house is in upscale Malibu, and a key stakeout is in Pasadena. For bungee jumping there's the

Vincent Thomas Bridge looming over L.A. harbor. Shipwreck Joey's Cabaret in San Pedro is featured prominently and the rogue cop's love interest resides in the derelict suburb of the strip club. While formally part of the City of Los Angeles, the port neighborhood of San Pedro hangs like an appendix connected to the rest of the city by a slender corridor defined by the Harbor Freeway. In *Chinatown*, Jake Gittes goes to 'Pedro to get a replacement vehicle.

In *Pulp Fiction* (1995), and its unofficial sequel

Left: Cody Jarrett (James Cagney) proclaims, "Top of the World, Ma," before the South Bay storage tank explodes.

Top: Location at Santa Monica Pier used in *Farewell, My Lovely*.

Bottom: Marlowe (Robert Mitchum, lower left) meets his client Moose Malloy (Jack O'Halloran) at an arcade (set in Long Beach but shot in Santa Monica).

Jackie Brown (1997), writer/director Quentin Tarantino, who grew up in Los Angeles, details the decay of the 'burbs with quasi-operatic extravagance inspired by his stated favorite from the classic period, *Kiss Me Deadly. Pulp Fiction* interweaves several stories and multiple characters to create a neo-noir essay on darkness and corruption, an L.A. noir vision of drugs, racism, sadomasochism, and random violence amid the remnants of the dream in suburban Los Angeles.

Much of *Pulp Fiction* is shot in the San Fernando Valley, in the working class east end communities like North Hollywood and Pacoima, and in

Hawthorne in the South Bay. Tract houses are showing their age as are apartment buildings, like the one Butch the boxer (Bruce Willis) lives in and the slightly upscale abode in which the drugged-out youths who are trying to cheat the crime boss Marsellus (Ving Rhames) crash. All around are overcrowded, noisy spaces that now resemble projects more than the lower middle-class affordable units they were built to be decades earlier. Diners, no matter their names, but in particular the Hawthorne Grill which opens and closes the movie, are cut from the same mold as Chandler's "sleazy hamburger joints" with "sweaty greasy kitchens that would have poisoned a toad." In *Pulp Fiction*, these are easy marks for cut-rate stick-up artists, as are the strip malls full of liquor stores and donut shops or a car parts emporium, like the Autozone, which replaced the Hawthorne Grill a few years after the shooting of *Pulp Fiction*.

Cheap motels, often used for prostitution and drug orgies, also dot the landscape like the now-demolished Glen River Motel, where Butch and his girlfriend Fabienne (Maria de Medeiros) hide out. The boxing match he refuses to throw is shot in the derelict Olympic Auditorium and matched with an exterior at

Left: Vincent Thomas Bridge from San Pedro to Long Beach featured in *Heat* and *To Live and Die in L.A.*.

Right: Robbers "Honey Bunny" (Amanda Plummer) and "Pumpkin" (Tim Roth) conspire at the Hawthorne Grill (now an Autozone).

the Raymond Theater in Pasadena. Above the working-class tracts, the nouveau riche have gone into the hills above Ventura Boulevard or off Mulholland Drive, which is where drug king Marsellus and his addicted wife Mia (Uma Thurman) reside. Below in the wastelands of White trash are mom-and-pop stores run by angry Anglos, who feel disenfranchised and displaced by the influx of Latinos, Blacks, and Asians into their once red-lined neighborhoods. Tarantino epitomizes them in the character of the "redneck" owner of the Mason-Dixon Pawn Shop and its outlandish S&M dungeon in the rear, where the racist owner and his cop friend beat and rape hapless victims. It is into this torture chamber that Butch and the African-American Marsellus stumble while brawling in the streets.

The noir underworld is everywhere. Hitman Vincent (John Travolta) accompanies Mia to a theme restaurant, shot partially in Kendall Alley in Pasadena and then on a sound stage, where women touch up their faces in the bathroom and then bend down to snort cocaine. Vincent buys his heroin from a hippieish dealer named Lance (Eric Stoltz) who inhabits a small bungalow in the Echo Park area, where Vincent takes Mia after she overdoses. Even still affluent suburban communities like Toluca Lake are not safe. It is there that Vincent and his partner Jules (Samuel L. Jackson) invade the middle-class home of Jules' former friend Jimmie (Tarantino) after a hit goes wrong. Jimmie is frantic, not over the killing but at the

prospect of his wife returning and divorcing him if she finds a body in their garage.

Two Days in the Valley (1996), directed and written by John Herzfeld, covers much the same ground, literally and figuratively, as *Pulp Fiction* and shares its post-modern irony and twisted humor. It opens on Mulholland Drive overlooking the eastern part of the San Fernando Valley. The key difference between this movie and Tarantino's is that it focuses more specifically on the lives of the disaffected rich and famous. Herzfeld's characters are new millennium gentry, wealthy enough to afford spacious houses above the desert-like flatlands or at least chic retreats in upper middle-class complexes that stretch south of Ventura from Studio City to Encino and Tarzana. But even in these hills, there are "a thousand white houses built up and down the hills, ten thousand lighted windows and the stars hanging down over them politely," as Chandler wrote in *The High Window,* "not getting too close."

One character in *Two Days in the Valley* is ski champion Becky Foxx (Teri Hatcher), whose cheating husband Roy (Peter Horton) is murdered with her consent as part of an insurance scam in their woodsy Mulholland hideaway. Another is pretentious and abusive art dealer Hopper (Greg Cruttwell) whose Mulholland post-modern mansion becomes the tempo-

Hitman Dosmo (Danny Aiello, at right with gun) holds art dealer Allan Hopper (Greg Cruttwell) and his assistant Susan (Glenne Headly) hostage on a Mulholland Drive rooftop.

rary refuge for an aging New York hitman Dosmo Pizzo (Danny Aiello) with a pathological fear of dogs and an old-fashioned sense of honor.

The faux Tudor hotel on Ventura Boulevard in Tarzana houses the masterminds of the insurance scam: the psychopathic Lee Woods (James Spader) and his languorous lover Helga (Charlize Theron), described by Becky as a "Viking bitch." Woods' psychopathic analog on the other side of the law is L.A.P.D. detective Strayer (Jeff Daniels). Like the redneck owner of the pawn shop in *Pulp Fiction*, Strayer represents the shrinking White majority of the Valley who sees in every immigrant and in every face of color an enemy, an invader ready, as he tells his idealistic partner Taylor (Eric Stoltz), to soil the image of the Valley and to take away his most prized possession, his small house in Studio City.

So Strayer forces his partner to entrap immigrant Vietnamese massage girls while he waits indignantly in his car in a strip mall in North Hollywood. Later Strayer even pulls a gun on an African-American golfer who accidentally hits a ball into the window of his beloved house. Even the characters who have fallen on hard times, like the suicidal screenwriter and director Teddy Peppers (played by actual writer/director Paul Mazursky) can embrace the dream, can envision themselves as just a twist of fate away from a comeback. Pepper's final "thank you" to Dosmo says as much, for the hitman has given him a possible idea for a new script. Hope springs eternal in the hills above the Valley.

Tarantino's *Jackie Brown* concentrates on the South Bay, where the writer/director was raised, and opens at the unofficial gateway to the area, LAX. In his typical obsessive style, Tarantino's camera lingers throughout the entire title sequence on the figure of Jackie Brown incarnated by Pam Grier, star of such blaxploitation, quasi-feminist action films of the seventies as *Coffy* and *Foxy Brown*. She glides through the airport like a female Marcellus or an African-American goddess fallen to earth. But the viewer soon discovers that this modern goddess has real life problems. She works as an underpaid flight attendant struggling to make a living after taking the fall for her drug-dealer husband.

San Fernando Valley looking west from the Burbank foothills in the 1980s.

Jackie lives in a cramped, low-rent apartment in Hawthorne, very near the famous Cockatoo Inn, the tacky apotheosis of the "suburban posh" where several scenes of the film are set. Victimized, like so many residents of that area, by a shrinking job market, Jackie needs to supplement her income and agrees to bring in money from Mexico for Ordell Robbie (Samuel L. Jackson). Although Ordell's home base is the ghettoized city of Compton, the middle-class South Bay is his stomping ground, a fertile market for drugs and guns.

Ordell spends most of his time with his girlfriend Melanie (Bridget Fonda) who has an apartment in Hermosa Beach. Melanie is a comic stereotype of the "surfer girl," the Valley Girl spin-off who populates the coastal towns of the South Bay. She is blonde, lithe, and shallow. She spends most of the film lounging in her bikini on the couch, watching TV, and doing drugs. When she does decide to take action and attempts to double cross Ordell and his dense partner Louis Gara (Robert De Niro), she fails miserably and pays the ultimate price of a neo-femme fatale. The other protagonist is Max Cherry (Robert Forster), an aging bail bonds-

Top: Jackie Brown (Pam Grier) meets Max Cherry (Robert Forster) in the food court of the Del Amo Fashion Center.

Right: *Jackie Brown* location, currently being partially demolished.

man, whose business has actually been boosted by the growing crime rate in the area. Tired of making money, Cherry forms an obsessed attachment to Jackie.

As important as any character in the movie is the Del Amo Fashion Center in Torrance, the largest such structure in the western United States. Like its sister malls scattered throughout the suburbs, Del Amo was designed to be a total entertainment center for the area's middle-class, offering chain stores, food courts, movie multiplexes, and arcades. But most importantly, the mall designers aspired to create an insular and safe environment: free of crime, pollution, and, of course, anything natural.

As the suburbs declined, so did their gathering places. Ironically, many of Tarantino's locations in *Pulp Fiction* and *Jackie Brown* have proved eminently disposable and have met the wrecking ball: not just the outmoded Cockatoo Inn (rebuilt after a fire in 1958) but even large portions of the Del Amo Fashion Center (built in 1975). Malls like this one became gang hangouts full of empty shops, tacky storefronts and second-rate movie houses. Much of the criminal planning and activity in *Jackie Brown* takes place in the mall. The characters meet in the food court and the shops to exchange contraband currency. Louis murders the whining Melanie in the parking lot. The government agents swarm over the brightly lit walkways to apprehend the perps. For neo-noir at the new millennium, the tarnished dream of the suburbs is all that remains. Flashy grifters have become simple lowlifes, and, unlike Cody Jarrett, nobody goes out on top of the world.

For many of the prototypical figures of film noir, Los Angeles or any urban landscape is home ground. Driven by a need to escape some dark part or to accomplish some dark task, many of these characters must venture away into unfamiliar terrain. For some, like the falsely accused James Vanning (Aldo Ray) in Jacques Tourneur's *Nightfall* (1957) or brutal cop Jim Wilson (Robert Ryan) in Nicholas Ray's *On Dangerous Ground* (1952), the voyage into the open country surrounding Los Angeles is short both in time

Jackie Brown **location, currently being demolished.**

and in distance but profoundly important in terms of the narrative and emotional deliverance.

There was a shift in noir cycle, beginning with pictures such as Jules Dassin's *The Naked City* (set in New York) and the Fox docu-noirs such as *Call Northside 777* (situated in Chicago) and even *Panic in the Streets* (set in New Orleans), in which spare black-and-white photography captured the same sort of everyday backgrounds from docks to high-rises to ethnic neighborhoods that exist somewhere in almost every metropolitan area. Director Don Siegel used the seamy underside of Los Angeles in *Private Hell 36* (1954), which ranges from tract homes and trailer parks to the racetrack as it follows two rogue detectives. The same year gas stations, industrial thoroughfares, and run-down apartments evoked the same sense of urban blight in Andre de Toth's *Crime Wave*. Three years later, Stanley Kubrick used the same progression across an urban landscape as he followed the criminal protagonists in *The Killing* (1957) without identifying the city itself. Whether Los Angeles portrayed itself or was merely an archetype for any urban area, both the filmmakers and the audience of classic period noir understood the shorthand, the association between setting and situation, between a figure in a noir landscape and a figure in a noir drama.

What the pictures which define the vision of L.A. noir demonstrate is the core influence of the urban setting which Los Angeles typified in the noir style, in the backstories of film noir's characters and in the visual choices of its directors. What these pictures also show is that L.A. noir, that particular dynamic between the vision begun in the classic period and the actual locales of the City of Angels, is a fluid and expressive milieu. L.A. noir is also open-ended. So long as pictures as diverse as *L.A. Confidential* and *Mulholland Drive* continue to incorporate the metropolis into the mix, continue to use the city as character, L.A. noir will continue to evolve.

Present day view of a location from *Crimson Kimono*; the diagonal street that cut between First and Second towards City Hall, now paved over and named after Japanese-American astronaut Onizuka.

L.A. NOIR Selected Bibliography

Other books on film noir written or edited by Alain Silver and James Ursini:

Film Noir: An Encyclopedic Reference to the American Style, Third Edition, edited by Elizabeth Ward and Alain Silver, co-edited by Robert Porfirio, Carl Macek, and James Ursini, New York: Overlook Press, 1979 (1st), 1987 (2nd), 1992 (3rd).

Film Noir Reader, New York: Limelight Editions, 1996.

Film Noir Reader 2, New York: Limelight Editions, 1999.

The Noir Style, New York: Overlook Press, 1999.

Film Noir Reader 3: Interviews with Filmmakers of the Classic Noir Period, edited with Robert Porfirio, New York: Limelight Editions, 2002.

Film Noir, London and Cologne: Taschen Books, 2004.

Film Noir Reader 4: The Crucial Films and Themes, New York: Limelight Editions, 2004.

Other books:

Borde, Raymond and Chaumeton, Étienne Chaumeton. *Panorama du Film Noir Americain, 1941-1953,* San Francisco: City Lights Books, 2002, translated by Paul Hammond.

Cameron, Ian, editor. *The Book of Film Noir,* New York; Continuum, 1993.

Caughey, John and LaRee, editors. *Los Angeles, Biography of a City,* Berkeley: University of California Press, 1976.

Ceplair, Larry and Englund, Steven. *The Inquisition in Hollywood,* Champaigne, Illinois, University of Illinois Press, 2003.

Christopher, Nicholas. *Somewhere in the Night: Film Noir and the American City,* New York: Henry Holt, 1997.

Davis, Mike. *City of Quartz: Excavating the Future in Los Angeles,* New York: Vintage, 1992.

Duncan, Paul. *Film Noir,* London: Pocket Essentials, 2001.

Durgnat, Raymond. *Luis Buñuel,* London: Studio Vista, 1967.

Gorman, Ed, Server, Lee and Greenberg, Martin, editors. *The Big Book of Noir,* New York: Carroll & Graf, 1998.

Huxley, Aldous. *Tomorrow and Tomorrow and Tomorrow,* New York: Harper & Row, 1956.

Kaplan, E. Ann, editor. *Women in Film Noir,* London: BFI Publishing, 1998 (Revised Edition).

Keyes, John D., editorial supervisor. *Los Angeles: A Guide to the City and its Environs,* New York: Hastings House, 1941.

McArthur, Colin. *Underworld U.S.A.,* New York: Viking Press, 1972.

Naremore, James. *More Than Night: Film Noir in its Contexts,* Berkeley: University of California Press, 1998.

Palmer, R. Barton. *Hollywood's Dark Cinema: the American Film Noir,* New York: Twayne Publishers, 1994.

_____, editor, *Perspectives on Film Noir,* New York: G.K. Hall, 1996.

Porfirio, Robert. *The Dark Age of American Film: A Study of American Film Noir (1940-1960),* Unpublished Doctoral Dissertation, Yale University, 1979.

Telotte, J. P. *Voices in the Dark: The Narrative Patterns of Film Noir,* Urbana, Illinois: University of Illinois Press, 1989.

Thompson, Peggy and Usukawa, Saeko. *Hard-boiled: Great Lines From Classic Noir Films,* San Francisco: Chronicle Books, 1995.

Ward, Elizabeth and Silver, Alain. *Raymond Chandler's Los Angeles,* New York: Overlooks Press, 1987.

L.A. NOIR Selected Filmography

Blade Runner (1982, Ladd Co./Warner Bros.). Directed by Ridley Scott. Screenplay by Hampton Fancher, David Webb Peoples, Roland Kibbee, based on the novel *Do Androids Dream of Electric Sheep?* By Philip K. Dick. Produced by Michael Deeley. Executive Producers: Hampton Fancher, Brian Kelly, Jerry Perenchio, Run Run Shaw, Bud Yorkin. Original Music: Vangelis. Cinematography: Jordan Cronenweth. Editing: Terry Rawlings. Casting: Jane Feinberg, Mike Fenton, Marci Liroff. Production Design: Lawrence G. Paull. Cast: Harrison Ford (Rick Deckard), Rutger Hauer (Roy Batty), Sean Young (Rachael), Edward James Olmos (Gaff), M. Emmet Walsh (Bryant), Daryl Hannah (Pris), William Sanderson (J.F. Sebastian), Brion James (Leon), Joe Turkel (Tyrell), Joanna Cassidy (Zhora), James Hong (Hannibal Chew), Morgan Paull (Holden), Kevin Thompson (Bear), John Edward Allen (Kaiser), Hy Pyke (Taffey Lewis), Kimiko Hiroshige (Cambodian Lady), Bob Okazaki (Howie Lee), Carolyn DeMirjian (Saleslady).

Brother (2000, Bandai Visual/Little Brother/Office Kitano/ Recorded Picture Co./Tokyo FM Broadcasting). Written and Directed by Takeshi Kitano. Produced by Masayuki Mori, Jeremy Thomas. Original Music: Joe Hisaishi. Cinematography: Katsumi Yanagishima. Editing: Takeshi Kitano, Yoshinori Oota. Production Design: Norihiro Isoda. Cast: Takeshi Kitano (Aniki Yamamoto), Omar Epps (Denny), Kuroudo Maki (Ken), Masaya Kato (Shirase), Susumu Terajima (Kato), Royale Watkins (Jay), Lombardo Boyar (Mo), Ren Osugi (Harada), Ryo Ishibashi (Ishihara), James Shigeta (Sugimoto), Tatyana Ali (Latifa), Makoto Otake (Chief of Police), Kouen Okumura (Hanaoka), Naomasa Musaka (Hisamatsu), Rino Katase (Night Club Madame), Tetsuya Watari (Jinseikai Boss), Ren Murakami (Minamino), Joy Nakagawa (Marina), Wanda-Lee Evans (Denny's Mother), Tony Colitti (Roberto), Koyo Into (Nishida), Alan Garcia (Bellboy), Antwon Tanner (Colin), Joseph Ragno (Mafia Boss Rossi), Nynno Ahli (Oscar), Paul Feddersen (Limo Driver), Dan Gunther (Killer Waiter).

Chinatown (1974, Paramount). Directed by Roman Polanski. Screenplay by Robert Towne, Roman Polanski. Produced by Robert Evans. Original Music: Jerry Goldsmith. Cinematography: John A. Alonzo. Editing: Sam O'Steen. Casting: Jane Feinberg, Mike Fenton. Production Design: Richard Sylbert. Cast: Jack Nicholson (J. J. "Jake" Gittes), Faye Dunaway (Evelyn Cross Mulwray), John Huston (Noah Cross), Perry Lopez (Lt. Lou Escobar), John Hillerman (Russ Yelburton), Darrell Zwerling (Hollis I. Mulwray), Diane Ladd (Ida Sessions), Roy Jenson (Claude Mulvihill), Roman Polanski (Man with Knife), Richard Bakalyan (Det. Loach), Joe Mantell (Lawrence Walsh), Bruce Glover (Duffy), Nandu Hinds (Sophie), James O'Rear (Lawyer), James Hong (Kahn), Beulah Quo (Mulwray's Maid), Jerry Fujikawa (Mulwray's Gardener), Belinda Palmer (Katherine Mulwray Cross), Roy Roberts

(Mayor Bagby), Noble Willingham (Councilman), Elliott Montgomery (Councilman), Rance Howard (Irate Farmer at Council Meeting), George Justin (Barney), Doc Erickson (Banker at Barbershop), Fritzi Burr (Mulwray's Secretary).

The Crimson Kimono (1959, Columbia/Globe). Written, produced and directed by Samuel Fuller. Original Music: Harry Sukman. Cinematography: Sam Leavitt. Editing: Jerome Thoms. Art Direction: Robert Boyle, William E. Flannery. Costume Design: Bernice Pontrelli. Cast: Victoria Shaw (Christine Downs), Glenn Corbett (Detective Sergeant Charlie Bancroft), James Shigeta (Detective Joe Kojaku), Anna Lee (Mac), Paul Dubov (Casale), Jaclynne Greene (Roma), Neyle Morrow (Hansel), Gloria Pall (Sugar Torch), Barbara Hayden (Mother), George Yoshinaga (Willy Hidaka), Kaye Elhardt (Nun), Aya Oyama (Sister Gertrude), George Okamura (Charlie, Karate Teacher), Reverend Ryosho S. Sogabe (Priest), Bob Okazaki (George Yoshinaga), Fuji ("Karate" Shuto).

Criss Cross (1949, Universal International). Directed by Robert Siodmak. Screenplay by Daniel Fuchs, based on the novel by Don Tracy. Produced by Michael Kraike. Original Music: Miklós Rózsa. Cinematography: Franz Planer. Editing: Ted J. Kent. Art Direction: Bernard Herzbrun, Boris Leven. Costume Design: Yvonne Wood. Cast: Burt Lancaster (Steve Thompson), Yvonne De Carlo (Anna Dundee), Dan Duryea (Slim Dundee), Stephen McNally (Det. Lt. Pete Ramirez),

Richard Long (Slade Thompson), Tom Pedi (Vincent), Percy Helton (Frank), Alan Napier (Finchley), Griff Barnett (Pop), Meg Randall (Helen, Slade's Fiancée), Joan Miller (Drunk at Roundup Bar), Edna Holland (Mrs. Thompson), John Doucette (Walt), Marc Krah (Mort), James O'Rear (Waxie), John "Skins" Miller (Midget), Esy Morales (Orchestra Leader).

D.O.A. (1950, Cardinal Pictures/United Artists). Directed by Rudolph Maté. Screenplay by Russell Rouse and Clarence Greene. Produced by Leo C. Popkin. Executive Producer: Harry M. Popkin. Original Music: Dimitri Tiomkin. Cinematography: Ernest Laszlo. Editing: Arthur H. Nadel. Art Direction: Duncan Cramer. Costume Design: Maria Donovan. Cast: Edmond O'Brien (Frank Bigelow), Pamela Britton (Paula Gibson), Luther Adler (Majak), Beverly Garland (Miss Foster), Lynn Baggett (Mrs. Philips), William Ching (Halliday), Henry Hart (Stanley Philips), Neville Brand (Chester), Laurette Luez (Marla Rakubian), Jess Kirkpatrick (Sam), Cay Forrester (Sue), Fred Jaquet (Dr. Matson), Lawrence Dobkin (Dr. Schaefer), Frank Gerstle (Dr. MacDonald), Carol Hughes (Kitty), Michael Ross (Dave), Donna Sanborn (Nurse).

Devil in a Blue Dress (1995, Mundy Lane/Tristar/Clinica Estetico/Columbia). Directed by Carl Franklin. Screenplay by Carl Franklin, based on the novel by Walter Mosley. Produced by Jesse Beaton, Gary Goetzman. Associate Producer: Walter

Mosley, Executive Producers: Jonathan Demme, Edward Saxon. Original Music: Elmer Bernstein. Cinematography: Tak Fujimoto. Editing: Carole Kravetz. Casting: Victoria Thomas. Production Design: Gary Frutkoff. Costume Design: Sharen Davis. Cast: Denzel Washington (Ezekiel "Easy" Rawlins), Tom Sizemore (DeWitt Albright), Jennifer Beals (Daphne Monet), Don Cheadle (Raymond "Mouse" Alexander), Maury Chaykin (Matthew Terell), Terry Kinney (Todd Carter), Mel Winkler (Joppy), Albert Hall (Degan Odell), Lisa Nicole Carson (Coretta James), Jernard Burks (Dupree Brouchard), David Wolos-Fonteno (Junior Fornay), John Roselius (Detective Mason), Beau Starr (Detective Miller), Steven Randazzo (Benny Giacomo), Scott Lincoln (Richard McGee), L. Scott Caldwell (Hattie May Parsons), Barry Shabaka Henley (Woodcutter),

Nick Corello (Sheriff), Kenny Endoso (Manny), Joseph Latimore (Frank Green), Renée Humphrey (Barbara), R.J. Knoll (Herman), Kai Lennox (Football), Poppy Montgomery (Barbara's Sister), Brendan Kelly (Norman), Peggy Rea (Carter's Secretary), Vinny Argiro (Baxter), Deborah Lacey (Sophie), Brazylia Kotere (Neighborhood Woman), Jeris Poindexter (Alphonso Jenkins), Frank Davis (Butcher), Matthew Barry (Cop in Car), Mark Cotone (Cop in Station), Brian E. O'Neal (John's Band/Singer), G. Smokey Campbell (Nightclub Owner), Alan Craig Schwartz (Johnny), Steve Sekely (Abe), J.D. Smith (Pool Hall Owner), Nigel Gibbs (Bootlegger).

Double Indemnity (1944, Paramount). Directed by Billy Wilder. Screenplay by Billy Wilder and Raymond Chandler, based on the novella by James M. Cain. Produced by Joseph Sistrom. Executive Producer: Buddy G. DeSylva. Original Music: Miklós Rózsa. Cinematography: John F. Seitz. Editing: Doane Harrison. Art Direction: Hans Dreier, Hal Pereira. Costume Design: Edith Head. Cast: Fred MacMurray (Walter Neff), Barbara Stanwyck (Phyllis Dietrichson), Edward G. Robinson (Barton Keyes), Porter Hall (Mr. Jackson), Jean Heather (Lola Dietrichson), Tom Powers (Mr. Dietrichson), Byron Barr (Nino Zachetti), Richard Gaines (Edward S. Norton, Jr.), Fortunio Bonanova (Sam Garlopis), John Philliber (Joe Peters).

The Driver (1978, 20th Century-Fox). Written and directed by Walter Hill. Produced by Lawrence Gordon. Original Music: Michael Small. Cinematography: Philip H. Lathrop. Editing:

Tina Hirsch, Robert K. Lambert. Casting by Jane Feinberg, Mike Fenton. Production Design: Harry Horner. Cast: Ryan O'Neal (The Driver), Bruce Dern (The Detective), Isabelle Adjani (The Player), Ronee Blakley (The Connection), Matt Clark (Red Plainclothesman), Felice Orlandi (Gold Plainclothesman), Joseph Walsh (Glasses), Rudy Ramos (Teeth), Denny Macko (Exchange Man), Frank Bruno (The Kid), Will Walker (Fingers), Sandy Brown Wyeth (Split), Tara King (Frizzy), Richard Carey (Floorman), Fidel Corona (Card Player), Victor Gilmour (Boardman), Nick Dimitri (Blue Mask), Bob Minor (Green Mask), Angelo Lamonea (Patron), Patrick Burns (Patron), Karen Kleiman (Patron), Thomas Myers (Passenger), Bill McConnell (Passenger), Peter Jason (Commuter), William Hasley (Commuter), Allan Graf (Uniformed Cop).

Farewell, My Lovely (1975, EK/ITC). Directed by Dick Richards. Screenplay by David Zelag Goodman, based on the novel by Raymond Chandler. Produced by Jerry Bick, Jerry Bruckheimer, Elliott Kastner, George Pappas. Original Music: David Shire. Cinematography: John A. Alonzo. Film Editing: Joel Cox, Walter Thompson. Casting: Louis DiGiaimo. Production Design: Dean Tavoularis. Costume Design: G. Tony Scarano. Cast: Robert Mitchum (Philip Marlowe), Charlotte Rampling (Helen Grayle), John Ireland (Lt. Nulty), Sylvia Miles (Mrs. Florian), Anthony Zerbe (Brunette), Harry Dean Stanton (Billy Rolfe), Jack O'Halloran (Moose Malloy), Joe Spinell (Nick), Sylvester Stallone (Kelly/Jonnie), Kate Murtagh (Amthor), John O'Leary (Marriott), Walter McGinn

(Tommy Ray), Burton Gilliam (Cowboy), Jim Thompson (Mr. Grayle), Jimmy Archer (Georgie), Ted Gehring (Roy), Logan Ramsey (Commissioner), Margie Hall (Woman), Jack Bernardi (Louis Levine), Bennett Ohta (Patron in Pool Hall), Jerry Fujikawa (Fence), Richard Kennedy (Detective #1), John O'Neil (Detective #2), Mark Allen (Detective #3), Andrew Harris (Mulatto Child), Napoleon Whiting (Hotel Clerk), John Eames (Butler), Cheryl Smith (Doris), Stu Gilliam (Man).

Gun Crazy (aka *Deadly is the Female*, 1950, King Bros./Pioneer Pictures/UA). Directed by Joseph H. Lewis. Screenplay by Millard Kaufman, Dalton Trumbo [uncredited], MacKinlay Kantor, based on his story. Produced by

Frank King. Maurice King. Original Music: Victor Young. Cinematography: Russell Harlan. Editing: Harry Gerstad. Production Design: Gordon Wiles. Costume Design: Norma Koch. Cast: Peggy Cummins (Annie Laurie Starr), John Dall (Bart Tare), Berry Kroeger (Packett), Morris Carnovsky (Judge Willoughby), Anabel Shaw (Ruby Tare), Harry Lewis (Sheriff Clyde Boston), Nedrick Young (Dave Allister), Russ Tamblyn (Bart Tare, Age 14).

Heat (1995, Forward Pass/Monarchy/Regency/Warner Bros.). Written and Directed by Michael Mann. Produced by Art Linson, Michael Mann. Executive Producers: Arnon Milchan, Pieter Jan Brugge. Original Music: Michael Brook, Brian Eno, Elliot Goldenthal, Moby (songs "New Dawn Fades" and "God Moving Over the Face of the Waters"), Terje Rypdal. Cinematography: Dante Spinotti. Editing: Pasquale Buba, William Goldenberg, Dov Hoenig, Tom Rolf. Casting: Bonnie Timmermann. Production Design: Neil Spisak. Costume Design: Deborah L. Scott. Cast: Al Pacino (Lt. Vincent Hanna), Robert De Niro (Neil McCauley), Val Kilmer (Chris Shiherlis), Jon Voight (Nate), Tom Sizemore (Michael Cheritto), Diane Venora (Justine Hanna), Amy Brenneman (Eady), Ashley Judd (Charlene Shiherlis), Mykelti Williamson (Sergeant Drucker), Wes Studi (Detective Casals), Ted Levine (Bosko), Dennis Haysbert (Donald Breedan), William Fichtner (Roger Van Zant), Natalie Portman (Lauren Gustafson), Tom Noonan (Kelso), Kevin Gage (Waingro), Hank Azaria (Alan Marciano), Susan Traylor (Elaine Cheritto), Kim Staunton (Lillian), Danny Trejo (Trejo), Henry Rollins (Hugh Benny), Jerry Trimble (Schwartz), Martin Ferrero (Construction Clerk), Ricky Harris (Albert Torena), Tone Loc (Richard Torena).

Hickey & Boggs (1972, MGM/UA). Directed by Robert Culp. Screenplay by Walter Hill. Produced by Fouad Said. Original Music: Ted Ashford; George Edwards (song "Hickey and Boggs"). Cinematography: Bill Butler. Editing: David Berlatsky. Casting: Lynn Stalmaster. Costume Design: William Ware Theiss. Cast: Bill Cosby (Al Hickey), Robert Culp (Frank Boggs), Ta-Ronce Allen (Nyona's Daughter), Rosalind Cash (Nyona), Lou Frizzell (Lawyer), Nancy Howard (Apartment Manager's Wife), Bernard Nedell (Used Car Salesman), Isabel Sanford (Nyona's Mother), Sheila Sullivan (Edith Boggs), Carmen (Mary Jane), Jason Culp (Mary Jane's Son), Ron Henriquez (Florist), Louis Moreno (Quemando), Caryn Sanchez (Mary Jane's Daughter), Robert Mandan (Mr. Brill), Michael Moriarty (Ballard), Denise Renfro (Brill's Daughter), Bernie Schwartz (Bernie), Matt Bennett (Fatboy), Bill Hickman (Monte), Gerald Peters (Jack), Tom Signorelli (Nick), Keri Shuttleton (Playground Kid), Wanda Spell (Playground Kid), Winston Spell (Playground Kid), Jack Colvin (Shaw), Vincent Gardenia (Papadakis), Ed Lauter (Ted), Joe E. Tata (Coroner's Assistant), James Woods (Lieutenant Wyatt), Lester Fletcher (Rice).

Impulse (1990, Warner Bros.). Directed by Sondra Locke. Screenplay by John DeMarco, Leigh Chapman. Produced by André E. Morgan, Albert S. Ruddy. Executive Producer: Dan Kolsrud. Original Music: Michel Colombier. Cinematography:

Dean Semler. Editing: John W. Wheeler. Casting: Glenn Daniels. Production Design: William A. Elliott. Costume Design: Deborah Hopper. Cast: Theresa Russell (Lottie Mason), Jeff Fahey (Stan), George Dzundza (Lt. Joe Morgan), Alan Rosenberg (Charley Katz), Nicholas Mele (Rossi), Eli Danker (Dimarjian), Charles McCaughan (Frank Munoff), Lynne Thigpen (Dr. Gardner), Shawn Elliott (Tony Peron), Angelo Tiffe (Luke), Christopher Lawford (Steve), Nick Savage (Edge), Dan Bell (Anson), Tom Dahlgren (District Attorney), Daniel Quinn (Ted Gates), David L. Crowley (Trick in Car), Mark Rolston (Man in Bar), Russell Curry (Bartender Mills), Pete Antico (Vice Cop in Bar), Karl Anthony Smith (Gas Station Attendant).

In a Lonely Place (1950, Santana/Columbia). Directed by Nicholas Ray. Screenplay by Edmund H. North, Andrew Solt, based on the novel by Dorothy B. Hughes. Produced by Robert Lord. Original Music: George Antheil. Cinematography: Burnett Guffey. Editing: Viola Lawrence. Art Direction: Robert Peterson. Costume Design: Jean Louis. Cast: Humphrey Bogart (Dixon Steele), Gloria Grahame (Laurel Gray), Frank Lovejoy (Det. Sgt. Brub Nicolai), Carl Benton Reid (Capt. Lochner), Art Smith (Mel Lippman), Jeff Donnell (Sylvia Nicolai), Martha Stewart (Mildred Atkinson), Robert Warwick (Charlie Waterman), Morris Ankrum (Lloyd Barnes), William Ching (Ted Barton), Steven Geray (Paul), Hadda Brooks (Singer).

Jackie Brown (1997, A Band Apart/Bender Productions/Mighty Mighty Afrodite/Miramax). Directed by Quentin Tarantino. Screenplay by Quentin Tarantino, based on the novel *Rum Punch* by Elmore Leonard. Produced by Lawrence Bender. Executive Producers: Richard N. Gladstein, Elmore Leonard, Bob Weinstein, Harvey Weinstein. Original Music: Joseph Julián González. Cinematography: Guillermo Navarro. Editing: Sally Menke. Casting: Jaki Brown, Robyn M. Mitchell. Production Design: David Wasco. Costume Design: Mary Claire Hannan. Cast: Pam Grier (Jackie Brown), Samuel L. Jackson (Ordell Robbie), Robert Forster (Max Cherry), Bridget Fonda (Melanie Ralston), Michael Keaton (Ray Nicolette), Robert De Niro (Louis Gara), Michael Bowen (Mark Dargus), Chris Tucker (Beaumont Livingston), Lisa Gay Hamilton (Sheronda), Tom "Tiny" Lister Jr. (Winston), Hattie Winston (Simone), Sid Haig (Judge), Aimee Graham (Amy, Billingsley Sales Girl), Ellis Williams (Cockatoo Bartender), Tangie Ambrose (Billingsley Sales Girl #2), T'Keyah Crystal Keymáh (Raynelle, Ordell's Junkie Friend), Venessia Valentino (Cabo Flight Attendant), Diana Uribe (Anita Lopez), Renee Kelly (Cocktail Waitress), Elizabeth McInerney (Bartender at Sam's), Colleen Mayne (Girl at Security Gate).

The Killing of a Chinese Bookie (1976, Faces Distributing). Written and directed by John Cassavetes. Produced by Al Ruban. Original Music: Bo Harwood. Cinematography: Mitch Breit, Al Ruban. Editing: Tom Cornwell. Production Design: Sam Shaw. Cast: Ben Gazzara (Cosmo Vitelli), Timothy Carey (Flo the Gangster), Seymour Cassel (Mort Weil), Robert Phillips (Phil), Morgan Woodward (John, the Head Gangster), John Kullers (Eddie), Al Ruban (Marty Reitz), Azizi Johari

(Rachel), Virginia Carrington (Betty, the Mother), Meade Roberts (Mr. Sophistication), Alice Fredlund (Sherry), Donna Gordon (Margo Donnar), Haji (Haji), Carol Warren (Carol), Derna Wong Davis (Derna), Kathalina Veniero (Annie), Yvette Morris (Yvette), Jack Ackerman (Musical Director), David Rowlands (Lamarr), Trisha Pelham (Waitress), Eddie Ike Shaw (Taxi Driver), Sonny Aprile (Sonny), Gene Darcy (Commodore), Ben Marino (Bartender), Arlene Allison (Waitress), Vincent Barbi (Vince), Val Avery (Blair Benoit), Elizabeth Deering (Lavinia), Hugo Soto (Chinese Bookie), Catherine Wong (The Bookie's Girl), John Finnegan (Taxi Driver), Miles Ciletti (Mickey).

Kiss Me Deadly (1955, Parklane Productions/United Artists). Produced and Directed by Robert Aldrich. Screenplay by A. I. Bezzerides, based on the novel by Mickey Spillane. Executive Producer: Victor Seville. Music: Frank DeVol. Song: "Rather Have the Blues," lyrics and music by Frank DeVol, sung by Nat "King" Cole. Editing: Michael Luciano. Casting: Jack Murton. Art Direction: William Glasgow. Cinematography: Ernest Laszlo. Cast: Ralph Meeker (Mike Hammer), Albert Dekker (Dr. Soberin), Paul Stewart (Carl Evello), Maxine Cooper (Velda), Gaby Rodgers (Gabrielle/Lily Carver), Wesley Addy (Pat Murphy), Juano Hernandez (Eddie Yeager), Nick Dennis (Nick), Cloris Leachman (Christina), Marian Carr (Friday), Jack Lambert (Sugar), Jack Elam (Charlie Max), Jerry Zinneman (Sammy), Percy Helton (Morgue Attendant), Fortunio Bonanova (Carmen Trivago), Silvio Minciotti (Old Mover), Leigh Snowden (Girl at Pool), Madi Comfort (Singer),

Art Loggins (Bartender), Robert Cornthwaite, James Seay (FBI Men), Mara McAfee (Nurse), James McCallian ("Super"), Jesslyn Fax (Mrs. "Super"), Mort Marshall (Ray Diker), Strother Martin (Truck Driver), Marjorie Bennett (Manager), Robert Sherman (Gas Station Man), Keith McConnell (Athletic Club Clerk), Paul Richards (Attacker), Allen Lee (William Mist), Eddie Real (Side Man).

L.A. Confidential (1997, Monarchy/Regency/Warner Bros.). Directed by Curtis Hanson. Screenplay by Brian Helgeland, Curtis Hanson, based on the novel by James Ellroy. Produced by Curtis Hanson, Arnon Milchan, Michael G. Nathanson. Executive Producers: Dan Kolsrud, David L. Wolper. Original Music: Jerry Goldsmith. Songs: Joe Bushkin, John DeVries ("Oh! Look at Me Now"); David Holt ("The Christmas Blues"). Cinematography: Dante Spinotti. Editing: Peter Honess. Casting: Mali Finn. Production Design: Jeannine Oppewall. Costume Design: Ruth Myers. Cast: Kevin Spacey (Sgt. Jack Vincennes), Russell Crowe (Officer Wendell "Bud" White), Guy Pearce (Det. Lt. Edmund Jennings Exley), James Cromwell (Capt. Dudley Liam Smith), Kim Basinger (Lynn Bracken), Danny DeVito (Sid Hudgens), David Strathairn (Pierce Morehouse Patchett), Ron Rifkin (Dist. Atty. Ellis Loew), Matt McCoy (Brett Chase), Paul Guilfoyle (Meyer Harris "Mickey" Cohen), Paolo Seganti (Johnny Stompanato), Elisabeth Granli (Mickey Cohen's Mambo Partner), Sandra Taylor (Mickey Cohen's Mambo Partner), Steve Rankin (Officer Arresting Mickey Cohen), Graham Beckel (Sgt. Richard Alex "Dick" Stensland), Allan Graf (Wife Beater), Precious Chong (Wife),

Symba Smith (Karen, Jack's Dancing Partner), Bob Clendenin (Reporter at Hollywood Station), Lennie Loftin (Photographer at Hollywood Station), Will Zahrn (Liquor Store Owner), Amber Smith (Susan Lefferts), Darrell Sandeen (Leland "Buzz" Meeks), Michael Warwick (Sid's Assistant).

The Long Goodbye (1973, E-K Corporation/Lions Gate Films/United Artists). Directed by Robert Altman. Screenplay by Leigh Brackett, based on the novel by Raymond Chandler. Produced by Jerry Bick. Executive Producer: Elliott Kastner. Original Music: John Williams. Cinematography: Vilmos Zsigmond. Editing: Lou Lombardo. Cast: Elliott Gould (Philip Marlowe), Nina Van Pallandt (Eileen Wade), Sterling Hayden (Roger Wade), Mark Rydell (Marty Augustine), Henry Gibson (Dr. Verringer), David Arkin (Harry), Jim Bouton (Terry Lennox), Warren Berlinger (Morgan), Jo Ann Brody (Jo Ann Eggenweiler), Stephen Coit (Det. Farmer), Jack Knight (Mabel), Pepe Callahan (Pepe), Vincent Palmieri (Vince), Pancho Córdova (Doctor), Enrique Lucero (Jefe), Rutanya Alda (Rutanya Sweet), Tammy Shaw (Dancer), Jack Riley (Riley), Ken Sansom (Colony Guard), Jerry Jones (Det. Green), John Davies (Det. Dayton), Rodney Moss (Supermarket Clerk), Sybil Scotford (Real Estate Lady), Herb Kerns (Herbie).

M (1952, Columbia/Superior Pictures). Directed by Joseph Losey. Screenplay by Leo Katcher, Norman Reilly Raine, and Waldo Salt based on a script by Fritz Lang and Thea von Harbou. Produced by Seymour Nebenzal. Original Music: Michel Michelet. Cinematography: Ernest Laszlo. Editing:

Edward Mann. Art Direction: Martin Obzina. Cast: David Wayne (Martin W. Harrow), Howard Da Silva (Inspector Carney), Martin Gabel (Charlie Marshall, Crime Boss), Luther Adler (Dan Langley), Steve Brodie (Lt. Becker), Raymond Burr (Pottsy), Glenn Anders (Riggert), Norman Lloyd (Sutro), Walter Burke (MacMahan), John Miljan (Blind Baloon Vendor), Roy Engel (Police Chief Regan), Janine Perreau (The Last Little Girl), Leonard Bremen (Lemke), Benny Burt (Jansen), Bernard Szold (Bradbury Bldg. Watchman), Robin Fletcher (Elsie Coster), Karen Morley (Mrs. Coster), Jim Backus (the Mayor), Jorja Curtright (Mrs. Stewart).

Mildred Pierce (1945, Warner Bros.). Directed by Michael Curtiz. Produced by Jerry Wald. Screenplay by Ranald MacDougall and [uncredited] Catherine Tunney, William Faulkner, based on the novel by James M. Cain. Original Music: Max Steiner. Cinematography: Ernest Haller. Editing: David Weisbart. Art Direction: Anton Grot. Costume Design: Milo Anderson. Cast: Joan Crawford (Mildred Pierce), Jack Carson (Wally Fay), Zachary Scott (Monty Beragon), Eve Arden (Ida Korvin), Ann Blyth (Veda Pierce), Bruce Bennett (Bert Pierce), Lee Patrick (Maggie Binderhof), Moroni Olsen (Inspector Peterson), Veda Ann Borg (Miriam Ellis), Jo Ann Marlowe (Kay Pierce), George Tobias (Mr. Chris), Barbara Brown (Mrs. Forrester), Charles Trowbridge (Mr. Williams), John Compton (Ted Forrester), Butterfly McQueen (Lottie), Garry Owen (Policeman on Pier), Joyce Compton (Waitress), Lynne Baggett (Waitress), Mary Servoss (Nurse), Manart Kippen (Doctor Gale), David Cota (Pancho).

Mulholland Drive (2001, Les Films Alain Sarde/ Asymmetrical Prods./Babbo/Le Studio Canal+/Picture Factory/Universal Focus). Written and directed by David Lynch. Produced by Neal Edelstein, Tony Krantz, Michael Polaire, Alain Sarde, Mary Sweeney. Executive Producer: Pierre Edelman. Original Music: Angelo Badalamenti; David Lynch, John Neff (additional music). Cinematography: Peter Deming. Editing: Mary Sweeney. Casting: Johanna Ray. Production Design: Jack Fisk. Costume Design: Amy Stofsky. Cast: Naomi Watts (Betty Elms/Diane Selwyn), Laura Harring (Rita/Camilla Rhodes), Ann Miller (Catherine "Coco" Lenoix), Dan Hedaya (Vincenzo Castigliane), Justin Theroux (Adam Kesher), Brent Briscoe (Detective Neal Domgaard), Robert Forster (Detective Harry McKnight), Katharine Towne (Cynthia Jenzen), Lee Grant (Louise Bonner), Scott Coffey (Wilkins), Billy Ray Cyrus (Gene), Chad Everett (Jimmy Katz), Rita Taggart (Linney James), James Karen (Wally Brown), Lori Heuring (Lorraine Kesher), Angelo Badalamenti (Luigi Castigliane), Michael Des Barres (Billy Deznutz), Marcus Graham (Vincent Darby), Missy Crider (Waitress at Winkies), Robert Katims (Ray Hott), Jeanne Bates (Irene), Dan Birnbaum (Irene's Companion at Airport), Scott Wulff (Limo Driver), Maya Bond (Ruth Elms), Patrick Fischler (Dan), Michael Cooke (Herb), Bonnie Aarons (Bum), Michael J. Anderson (Mr. Roque), Joseph Kearney (Roque's Manservant), Enrique Buelna (Back of Head Man), Richard Mead (Hairy-Armed Man), Sean Everett (Cab Driver at LAX), Daniel Rey (Valet Attendant), David Schroeder (Robert Smith), Tom Morris (Espresso Man), Melissa George (Camilla Rhodes), Matt Gallini (Castigliane Limo Driver),

Mark Pellegrino (Joe Messing), Vincent Castellanos (Ed), Diane Nelson (Heavy-Set Woman Killed by Messing), Charles Croughwell (Vacuum Man Killed by Messing), Rena Riffel (Laney), Tad Horino (Taka), Tony Longo (Kenny), Geno Silva (Cookie Park Hotel Manager/Club Silencio M.C.), Monty Montgomery (Cowboy), Kate Forster (Martha Johnson), Wayne Grace (Bob Brooker), Michele Hicks (Nicki Pelazza), Lisa K. Ferguson (Julie Chadwick), William Ostrander (2nd Assistant Director), Elizabeth Lackey (Carol), Brian Beacock (Backup Singer #1), Blake Lindsley (Backup Singer #2), Adrien Curry (Backup Singer #3), Tyrah M. Lindsey (Backup Singer #4), Michael D. Weatherred (Hank), Michael Fairman (Jason Goldwyn), Johanna Stein (Woman in #12), Richard Green (Bondar), Conte Candoli (Club Silencio Trumpet Player), Cori Glazer (Blue-Haired Lady in Balcony Seat at Club Silencio), Rebekah Del Rio (Herself), Christian Thompson (Dancer).

Night Has a Thousand Eyes (1948, Paramount). Directed by John Farrow. Screenplay by Barré Lyndon and Jonathan Latimer, based on the novel by Cornell Woolrich. Produced by Endre Bohem. Original Music: Victor Young. Cinematography: John F. Seitz. Editing: Eda Warren. Art Direction: Franz Bachelin, Hans Dreier. Costume Design: Edith Head. Cast: Edward G. Robinson (John Triton, "The Mental Wizard"), Gail Russell (Jean Courtland), John Lund (Elliott Carson), Virginia Bruce (Jenny Courtland), William Demarest (Lt. Shawn), Richard Webb (Peter Vinson), Jerome Cowan (Whitney Courtland), Onslow Stevens (Dr. Walters), John Alexander (Mr. Gilman), Roman Bohnen (Melville Weston), Luis Van

Rooten (Mr. Myers), Henry Guttman (Butler), Mary Adams (Miss Hendricks), Douglas Spencer (Dr. Ramsdell).

Pitfall (1948, Regal/United Artists). Directed by André De Toth. Screenplay by William Bowers, André De Toth, Karl Kamb, based on the novel by Jay Dratler. Produced by Samuel Bischoff. Music Director: Louis Forbes. Cinematography: Harry J. Wild. Editing: Walter Thompson. Art Direction: Arthur Lonergan. Cast: Dick Powell (John Forbes), Lizabeth Scott (Mona Stevens), Jane Wyatt (Sue Forbes), Raymond Burr (MacDonald), John Litel (District Attorney), Byron Barr (Bill Smiley), Jimmy Hunt (Tommy Forbes), Ann Doran (Maggie), Selmer Jackson (Ed Brawley), Margaret Wells (Terry), Dick Wessel (Desk Sergeant).

Pulp Fiction (1994, A Band Apart/Jersey Films/Miramax). Directed by Quentin Tarantino. Screenplay by Quentin Tarantino, from stories by Tarantino and Roger Avary. Produced by Lawrence Bender. Executive Producer: Danny DeVito, Richard N. Gladstein, Michael Shamberg, Stacey Sher, Bob Weinstein, Harvey Weinstein. Cinematography: Andrzej Sekula. Editing: Sally Menke. Casting by Ronnie Yeskel, Gary M. Zuckerbrod. Production Design: David Wasco. Costume Design: Betsy Heimann. Cast: John Travolta (Vincent Vega), Samuel L. Jackson (Jules Winnfield), Phil LaMarr (Marvin), Frank Whaley (Brett), Burr Steers (Roger), Bruce Willis (Butch Coolidge), Ving Rhames (Marsellus Wallace), Tim Roth ("Pumpkin"), Amanda Plummer ("Honey Bunny"), Laura Lovelace (Waitress), Paul Calderon (Paul), Bronagh Gallagher

(Trudi), Rosanna Arquette (Jody), Eric Stoltz (Lance), Uma Thurman (Mia Wallace), Jerome Patrick Hoban (Ed Sullivan), Michael Gilden (Phillip Morris Page), Gary Shorelle (Ricky Nelson), Susan Griffiths (Marilyn Monroe), Eric Clark (James Dean), Joseph Pilato (Dean Martin), Brad Parker (Jerry Lewis), Steve Buscemi (Buddy Holly), Lorelei Leslie (Mamie van Doren), Emil Sitka (Hold Hands You Lovebirds), Brenda Hillhouse (Butch's Mother), Christopher Walken (Capt. Koons), Chandler Lindauer (Young Butch), Sy Sher (Klondike), Robert Ruth (Sportscaster #1/Coffee Shop), Rich Turner (Sportscaster #2), Angela Jones (Esmarelda Villalobos), Don Blakely (Wilson's trainer), Carl Allen (Dead Floyd Wilson), Maria de Medeiros (Fabienne), Karen Maruyama (Gawker #1), Kathy Griffin (Herself), Venessia Valentino (Pedestrian/Bonnie Dimmick), Linda Kaye (Shot Woman), Duane Whitaker (Maynard), Peter Greene (Zed), Stephen Hibbert (The Gimp), Alexis Arquette (Man #4), Quentin Tarantino (Jimmie Dimmick), Harvey Keitel (Winston "The Wolf" Wolfe), Julia Sweeney (Raquel), Lawrence Bender (Long-Hair Yuppie Scum/"Zorro").

Quicksand (1950, Stiefel/United Artists). Directed by Irving Pichel. Screenplay by Robert Smith. Produced by Mort Briskin. Executive Producer: Samuel H. Stiefel. Original Music: Louis Gruenberg. Cinematography: Lionel Lindon. Editing: Walter Thompson. Production Design: Boris Leven. Cast: Mickey Rooney (Daniel Brady), Jeanne Cagney (Vera Novak), Barbara Bates (Helen Calder), Peter Lorre (Nick Dramoshag), Taylor Holmes (Harvey), Art Smith (Oren Mackey), Wally Cassell (Chuck Davis), Richard Lane (Det. Lt. Nelson), Patsy O'Connor (Millie), John Gallaudet (Moriarity), Minerva Urecal (Landlady).

Shockproof (1949, Columbia). Directed by Douglas Sirk. Screenplay by Helen Deutsch and Samuel Fuller. Produced by S. Sylvan Simon. Original Music: George Duning. Cinematography: Charles Lawton Jr. Editing: Gene Havlick. Art Direction: Carl Anderson. Costume Design: Jean Louis. Cast: Cornel Wilde (Griff Marat), Patricia Knight (Jenny Marsh), John Baragrey (Harry Wesson), Esther Minciotti (Mrs. Marat), Howard St. John (Sam Brooks), Russell Collins (Frederick Bauer), Charles Bates (Tommy Marat).

Sunset Boulevard (1950, Paramount). Directed by Billy Wilder. Screenplay by Charles Brackett, Billy Wilder, D.M. Marshman Jr. Produced by Charles Brackett. Original Music: Franz Waxman. Cinematography: John F. Seitz. Editing: Arthur Schmidt. Art Direction: Hans Dreier, John Meehan. Costume Design: Edith Head. Cast: William Holden (Joe Gillis), Gloria Swanson (Norma Desmond), Erich von Stroheim (Max von Mayerling), Nancy Olson (Betty Schaefer), Fred Clark (Sheldrake), Lloyd Gough (Morino), Jack Webb (Artie Green), Franklyn Farnum (Undertaker), Larry J. Blake (Finance Man #1), Charles Dayton (Finance Man #2), Cecil B. DeMille (Himself), Hedda Hopper (Herself), Buster Keaton (Card playing friend), Anna Q. Nilsson (Herself), H.B. Warner (Himself), Ray Evans (Himself), Jay Livingston (Himself).

COLUMBIA PICTURES presents CORNEL WILDE SHOCKPROOF with PATRICIA KNIGHT

T-Men (1947, Reliance Pictures/Eagle-Lion). Directed by Anthony Mann. Screenplay by John C. Higgins, based on the story by Virginia Kellogg. Produced by Aubrey Schenck. Original Music: Paul Sawtell. Cinematography: John Alton. Editing: Fred Allen. Art Direction: Edward C. Jewell. Cast: Dennis O'Keefe (Dennis O'Brien), Mary Meade (Evangeline), Alfred Ryder (Tony Genaro), Wallace Ford (the Schemer), June Lockhart (Mary Genaro), Charles McGraw (Moxie), Jane Randolph (Diana Simpson), Art Smith (Gregg), Herbert Heyes (Chief Carson), Jack Overman (Brownie), John Wengraf ("Shiv" Triano), Jim Bannon (Lindsay), William Malten (Paul Miller).

They Shoot Horses, Don't They? (1969, ABC/Palomar). Directed by Sydney Pollack. Screenplay by James Poe and

Robert E. Thompson, based on the novel by Horace McCoy. Produced by Robert Chartoff, Irwin Winkler. Executive Producer: Theodore B. Sills. Music Director: John Green. Cinematography: Philip H. Lathrop. Editing: Fredric Steinkamp. Casting: Lynn Stalmaster. Production Design: Harry Horner. Cast: Jane Fonda (Gloria), Michael Sarrazin (Robert), Susannah York (Alice), Gig Young (Rocky), Red Buttons (Sailor), Bonnie Bedelia (Ruby), Michael Conrad (Rollo), Bruce Dern (James), Al Lewis (Turkey), Robert Fields (Joel), Severn Darden (Cecil), Allyn Ann McLerie (Shirl), Madge Kennedy (Mrs. Laydon), Jacquelyn Hyde (Jackie), Felice Orlandi (Mario), Art Metrano (Max), Gail Billings (Lillian), Lynn Willis (Coley James), Maxine Greene (Agnes), Mary Gregory (Nurse), Robert Dunlap (College Boy), Paul Mantee (Jiggs), Tim Herbert (Doctor), Tom McFadden (Second Trainer).

This Gun for Hire (1942, Paramount). Directed by Frank Tuttle. Screenplay by Albert Maltz and W.R. Burnett, based on the novel *A Gun for Sale* by Graham Greene. Produced by Richard Blumenthal. Original Music: David Buttolph, Cinematography: John F. Seitz. Editing: Archie Marshek. Art Direction: Hans Dreier, Robert Usher. Costume Design: Edith Head. Cast: Veronica Lake (Ellen Graham), Robert Preston (Det. Lt. Michael Crane), Laird Cregar (Willard Gates), Alan Ladd (Philip Raven), Tully Marshall (Alvin Brewster), Marc Lawrence (Tommy, Gates' Chauffeur), Olin Howland (Blair Fletcher, Ellen's Agent), Roger Imhof (Sen. Burnett), Pamela Blake (Annie, Hotel Maid), Frank Ferguson (Albert Baker),

Victor Kilian (Drew, Brewster's Nurse), Patricia Farr (Ruby), Harry Shannon (Steve Finnerty), Charles C. Wilson (Police Captain), Mikhail Rasumny (Slukey, Carnival Game Operator), Bernadene Hayes (Baker's Secretary), Mary Davenport (Dress Salesgirl), Chester Clute (Stewart, Hotel Manager), Charles Arnt (Will Gates).

To Live and Die in L.A. (1985, New Century/MGM/UA). Directed by William Friedkin. Screenplay by William Friedkin and Gerald Petievich, based on the novel by Petievich. Produced by Irving H. Levin. Executive Producer: Samuel Schulman. Original Music: Darren Costin, Nick Feldman, Jack Hues (all as "Wang Chung"). Cinematography: Robby Müller. Editing: Bud S. Smith, M. Scott Smith. Casting: Robert Weiner. Production Design: Buddy Cone, Lilly Kilvert. Costume Design: Linda M. Bass. Cast: William L. Petersen (Richard Chance), Willem Dafoe (Eric "Rick" Masters), John Pankow (John Vukovich), Debra Feuer (Bianca Torres), John Turturro (Carl Cody), Darlanne Fluegel (Ruth Lanier), Dean Stockwell (Bob Grimes), Steve James (Jeff Rice), Robert Downey Sr. (Thomas Bateman), Michael Greene (Jim Hart), Christopher Allport (Max Waxman), Jack Hoar (Jack), Valentin de Vargas (Judge Filo Cedillo), Dwier Brown (Doctor), Michael Chong (Thomas Ling), Jackie Giroux (Claudia Leith), Michael Zand (Terrorist), Bobby Bass (FBI Agent), Dar Robinson (FBI Agent), Anne Betancourt (Nurse), Katherine M. Louie (Ticket Agent), Edward Harrell (Airport Guard), Gilbert Espinoza (Bartender), John Petievich (Agent), Zarko Petievich (Agent), Rick Dalton (Agent), Richard L. Lane (Agent), Jack Cota (Agent), Shirley J.

White (Airline Passenger), Gerald H. Brownlee (Visiting Room Guard), David M. DuFriend (Tower Guard), Rubén García (Inmate Ruben), Joe Duran (Prison Guard).

Touch of Evil (1958, Universal International). Directed by Orson Welles. Screenplay by Orson Welles and [uncredited: reshoots/added scenes] Paul Monash, Franklin Coen, based on the novel *Badge of Evil* by Whit Masterson. Produced by Albert Zugsmith. Original Music: Henry Mancini. Cinematography: Russell Metty. Editing: Aaron Stell, Virgil Vogel. Art Direction: Robert Clatworthy, Alexander Golitzen. Cast: Charlton Heston (Ramon Miguel "Mike" Vargas), Janet Leigh (Susan Vargas), Orson Welles (Police Captain Hank Quinlan), Joseph Calleia (Police Sergeant Pete Menzies), Akim Tamiroff ("Uncle" Joe Grandi), Joanna Moore (Marcia Linnekar), Ray Collins (District Attorney Adair), Marlene Dietrich (Tanya), Dennis Weaver (Mirador Motel Night Manager), Valentin de Vargas (Pancho, Grandi Hood), Mercedes McCambridge (Female Gang Leader), Mort Mills (Al Schwartz, District Attorney's Assistant), Victor Milian (Manolo Sanchez), Lalo Rios (Risto, Grandi's nephew throwing acid), Michael Sargent (Pretty Boy), Phil Harvey (Blaine), Joi Lansing (Blonde), Harry Shannon (Chief Gould), Zsa Zsa Gabor (Strip-Club Owner), Joseph Cotton (Surgeon) Keenan Wynn (Man).

2 Days in the Valley (1996, MGM). Written and Directed by John Herzfeld. Produced by Herb Nanas, Jeff Wald. Original Music: Anthony Marinelli. Cinematography: Oliver Wood. Editing: Jim Miller, Wayne Wahrman. Casting: Mindy Marin, John Papsidera. Production Design: Catherine Hardwicke. Costume Design: Betsy Heimann. Cast: Danny Aiello (Dosmo Pizzo), Greg Cruttwell (Allan Hopper), Jeff Daniels (Alvin Strayer), Teri Hatcher (Becky Foxx), Glenne Headly (Susan Parish), Peter Horton (Roy Foxx), Marsha Mason (Audrey Hopper), Paul Mazursky (Teddy Peppers), James Spader (Lee Woods), Eric Stoltz (Wes Taylor), Charlize Theron (Helga Svelgen), Keith Carradine (Detective Creighton), Louise Fletcher (Evelyn), Austin Pendleton (Ralph Crupi), Kathleen Luong (Midori), Michael Jai White (Buck), Cress Williams (Golfer), Lawrence Tierney (Older Man), Micole Mercurio (Older Woman), William Stanton (Man at Bar), Deborah Benson-Wald (Driver's Friend), Ada Maris (Detective Carla Valenzuela).

White Heat (1949, Warner Bros.). Directed by Raoul Walsh. Screenplay by Ivan Goff and Ben Roberts, based on the story by Virginia Kellogg. Produced by Louis F. Edelman. Original Music: Max Steiner. Editing: Owen Marks. Art Direction: Edward Carrere. Costume Design: Leah Rhodes. Cinematography: Sidney Hickox. Cast: James Cagney (Arthur "Cody" Jarrett), Virginia Mayo (Verna Jarrett), Edmond O'Brien (Vic Pardo/Hank Fallon), Margaret Wycherly (Ma Jarrett), Steve Cochran (Big Ed Somers), John Archer (Philip Evans), Wally Cassell (Giovanni "Cotton" Valletti), Fred Clark (Daniel Winston, "The Trader").

The photographs on pages 2–3, 7, 14–5, 41, 60–61, 93, 107, 129, 141, and 152 are Copyright © 1983–1986, Elizabeth Ward and Alain Silver.

Pages 2–3: Night vista from Lockheed View Drive in the Verdugo Mountains overlooking Burbank.

Pages 4–5: South side of Chung King Court also know as Old Chinatown Plaza, near Hill and College Streets in downtown Los Angeles.

Page 7: Interior entrance of Bradbury Building, 304 South Broadway.

Pages 10–11: View from the Sixth Street Bridge back towards downtown.

Pages 14–15: View from North Spring Street.

Page 19: View from the southwest corner of Wilshire Boulevard and LaFayette Park.

Page 20: House at 6301 Quebec Drive. Photo by India Brookover-Coleman.

Page 24: Chateau Marmont, 8221 Sunset Boulevard.

Page 32: View from the corner of Wilshire Boulevard and Fairfax Avenue.

Page 36: 1851 North Ivar Street.

Page 41: This gate was once at the intersection of Bronson and Marathon, but it is now located inside the Paramount lot just north of Melrose.

Page 43: Southeast corner of Fountain and La Brea Avenues.

Page 44: High Tower Drive north of Camrose Drive, Hollywood.

Page 45: View from the southeast corner of Sunset Boulevard at Las Palmas in Hollywood.

Page 47: 7156 Santa Monica Boulevard.

Page 49(a): Frolic Room, 6245 Hollywood Boulevard just east of Vine Street in Hollywood.

Page 49(b): Crossroads of the World, 6671 Sunset Boulevard just east of Las Palmas in Hollywood.

Page 50: 6525 Sunset Boulevard, Hollywood.

Page 51: 2912 Griffith Park Boulevard.

Page 53: 1016 West El Segundo Blvd, Gardena.

Page 54: View south from Mulholland Drive just east of Outpost Drive.

Page 55: 802 South Broadway. Photo by Linda Brookover.

Page 60(a): Carousel at Santa Monica pier on Appian Way just north of Moss Avenue, Santa Monica.

Page 60(b): View south from Will Rogers State Beach on Pacific Coast Highway just south of Sunset Boulevard.

Page 61: Entrance to the Santa Monica pier at Colorado Street and Ocean Avenue.

Page 68: Court apartments on Harper Avenue just north of Fountain, West Hollywood.

Page 71: Doheny Road just north of Sunset Boulevard in Beverly Hills.

Page 72: 10401 Wilshire Boulevard, West Los Angeles.

Page 76: Grand Canal, Venice in the 1950s, from the Security Pacific Bank Collection, Los Angeles Public Library.

Page 78: View southwest from Palisades Park, near Ocean Avenue and San Vicente Boulevard, Santa Monica.

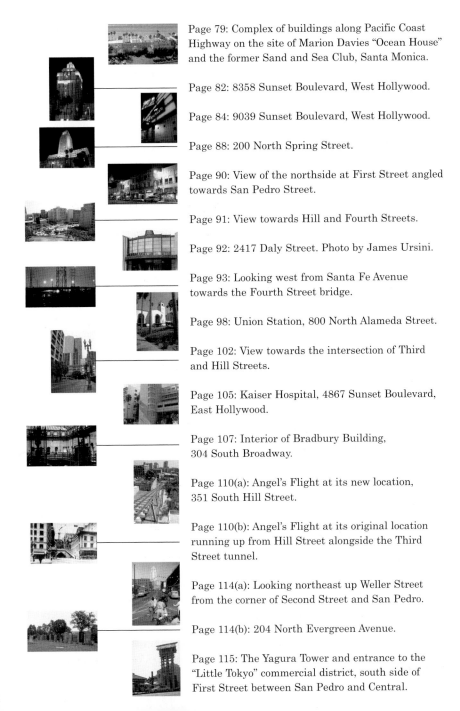

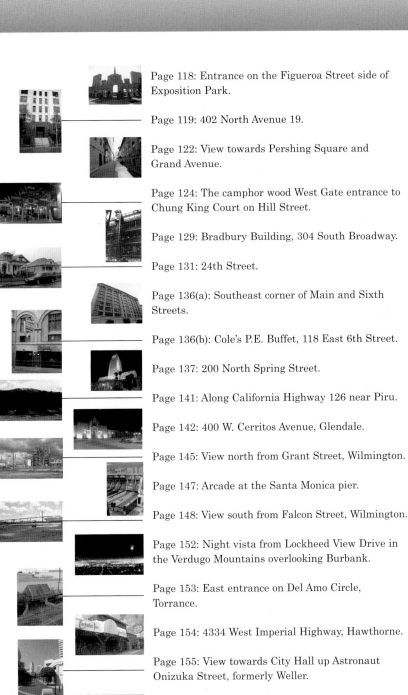

Page 79: Complex of buildings along Pacific Coast Highway on the site of Marion Davies "Ocean House" and the former Sand and Sea Club, Santa Monica.

Page 82: 8358 Sunset Boulevard, West Hollywood.

Page 84: 9039 Sunset Boulevard, West Hollywood.

Page 88: 200 North Spring Street.

Page 90: View of the northside at First Street angled towards San Pedro Street.

Page 91: View towards Hill and Fourth Streets.

Page 92: 2417 Daly Street. Photo by James Ursini.

Page 93: Looking west from Santa Fe Avenue towards the Fourth Street bridge.

Page 98: Union Station, 800 North Alameda Street.

Page 102: View towards the intersection of Third and Hill Streets.

Page 105: Kaiser Hospital, 4867 Sunset Boulevard, East Hollywood.

Page 107: Interior of Bradbury Building, 304 South Broadway.

Page 110(a): Angel's Flight at its new location, 351 South Hill Street.

Page 110(b): Angel's Flight at its original location running up from Hill Street alongside the Third Street tunnel.

Page 114(a): Looking northeast up Weller Street from the corner of Second Street and San Pedro.

Page 114(b): 204 North Evergreen Avenue.

Page 115: The Yagura Tower and entrance to the "Little Tokyo" commercial district, south side of First Street between San Pedro and Central.

Page 118: Entrance on the Figueroa Street side of Exposition Park.

Page 119: 402 North Avenue 19.

Page 122: View towards Pershing Square and Grand Avenue.

Page 124: The camphor wood West Gate entrance to Chung King Court on Hill Street.

Page 129: Bradbury Building, 304 South Broadway.

Page 131: 24th Street.

Page 136(a): Southeast corner of Main and Sixth Streets.

Page 136(b): Cole's P.E. Buffet, 118 East 6th Street.

Page 137: 200 North Spring Street.

Page 141: Along California Highway 126 near Piru.

Page 142: 400 W. Cerritos Avenue, Glendale.

Page 145: View north from Grant Street, Wilmington.

Page 147: Arcade at the Santa Monica pier.

Page 148: View south from Falcon Street, Wilmington.

Page 152: Night vista from Lockheed View Drive in the Verdugo Mountains overlooking Burbank.

Page 153: East entrance on Del Amo Circle, Torrance.

Page 154: 4334 West Imperial Highway, Hawthorne.

Page 155: View towards City Hall up Astronaut Onizuka Street, formerly Weller.

Page 170–172: Looking down First Street from the corner of San Pedro.

Judge John Aiso ←
San Pedro →

First St. between Alameda and San Pedro.

Books Available from Santa Monica Press

www.santamonicapress.com • 1-800-784-9553